Tauchlogbuch
divelog

© 2011 André Schubert. Alle Rechte vorbehalten.
ISBN 978-1-4475-9133-7

Persönliche Daten Personal Data

Vorname first name

Nachname last name

Geburtsdatum date of birth

Adresse address

PLZ, Ort zip, city

Land country

Telefon phone

E-Mail e-mail

Im Notfall zu benachrichtigen contact in case of emergency

Photo

Stempel stamp

Brevets certifications

Brevet certification	Ort location	Datum date

Ausrüstung equipment

Typ / type
Hersteller / manufacturer
Modell / model
Datum / date
Händler / dealer
Kaufpreis / price

Typ / type
Hersteller / manufacturer
Modell / model
Datum / date
Händler / dealer
Kaufpreis / price

Typ / type
Hersteller / manufacturer
Modell / model
Datum / date
Händler / dealer
Kaufpreis / price

Typ / type
Hersteller / manufacturer
Modell / model
Datum / date
Händler / dealer
Kaufpreis / price

Typ / type
Hersteller / manufacturer
Modell / model
Datum / date
Händler / dealer
Kaufpreis / price

Typ / type
Hersteller / manufacturer
Modell / model
Datum / date
Händler / dealer
Kaufpreis / price

Ausrüstung equipment

Typ
type
Hersteller
manufacturer
Modell
model

Datum
date
Händler
dealer
Kaufpreis
price

Typ
type
Hersteller
manufacturer
Modell
model

Datum
date
Händler
dealer
Kaufpreis
price

Typ
type
Hersteller
manufacturer
Modell
model

Datum
date
Händler
dealer
Kaufpreis
price

Typ
type
Hersteller
manufacturer
Modell
model

Datum
date
Händler
dealer
Kaufpreis
price

Typ
type
Hersteller
manufacturer
Modell
model

Datum
date
Händler
dealer
Kaufpreis
price

Typ
type
Hersteller
manufacturer
Modell
model

Datum
date
Händler
dealer
Kaufpreis
price

Ausrüstung equipment

Typ / type
Hersteller / manufacturer
Modell / model
Datum / date
Händler / dealer
Kaufpreis / price

Typ / type
Hersteller / manufacturer
Modell / model
Datum / date
Händler / dealer
Kaufpreis / price

Typ / type
Hersteller / manufacturer
Modell / model
Datum / date
Händler / dealer
Kaufpreis / price

Typ / type
Hersteller / manufacturer
Modell / model
Datum / date
Händler / dealer
Kaufpreis / price

Typ / type
Hersteller / manufacturer
Modell / model
Datum / date
Händler / dealer
Kaufpreis / price

Typ / type
Hersteller / manufacturer
Modell / model
Datum / date
Händler / dealer
Kaufpreis / price

Notizen notes

Notizen notes

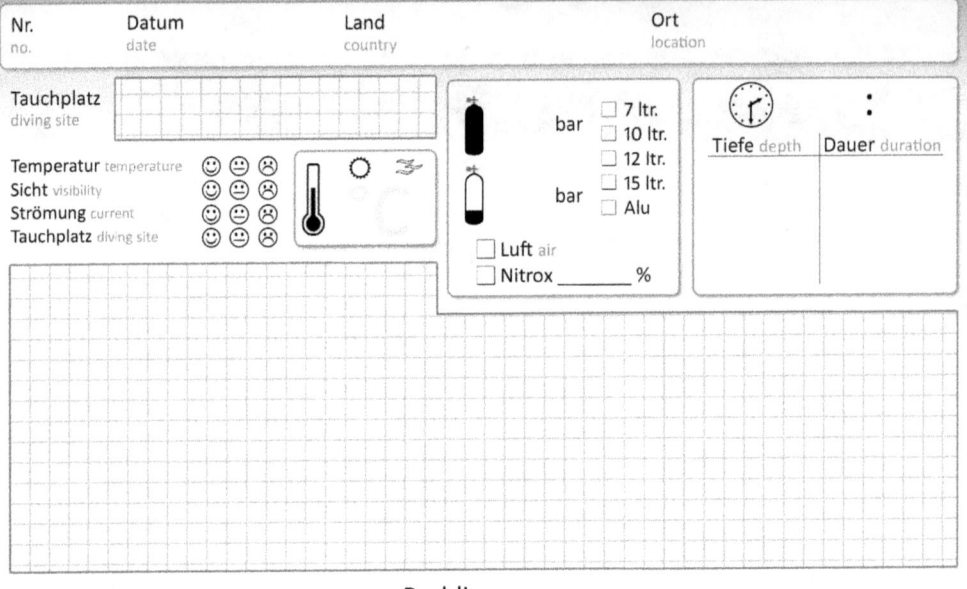

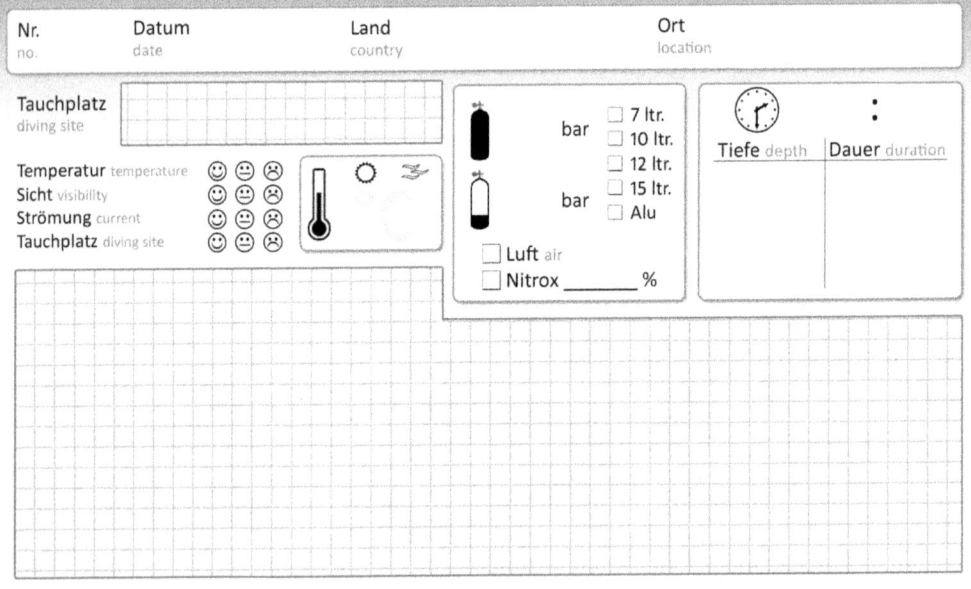

Nr. no.	Datum date	Land country		Ort location	

Tauchplatz diving site

Temperatur temperature ☺ 😐 ☹
Sicht visibility ☺ 😐 ☹
Strömung current ☺ 😐 ☹
Tauchplatz diving site ☺ 😐 ☹

bar
bar
☐ 7 ltr.
☐ 10 ltr.
☐ 12 ltr.
☐ 15 ltr.
☐ Alu
☐ Luft air
☐ Nitrox _____ %

Tiefe depth | Dauer duration

Instructor
Signature:

Buddies

No.:

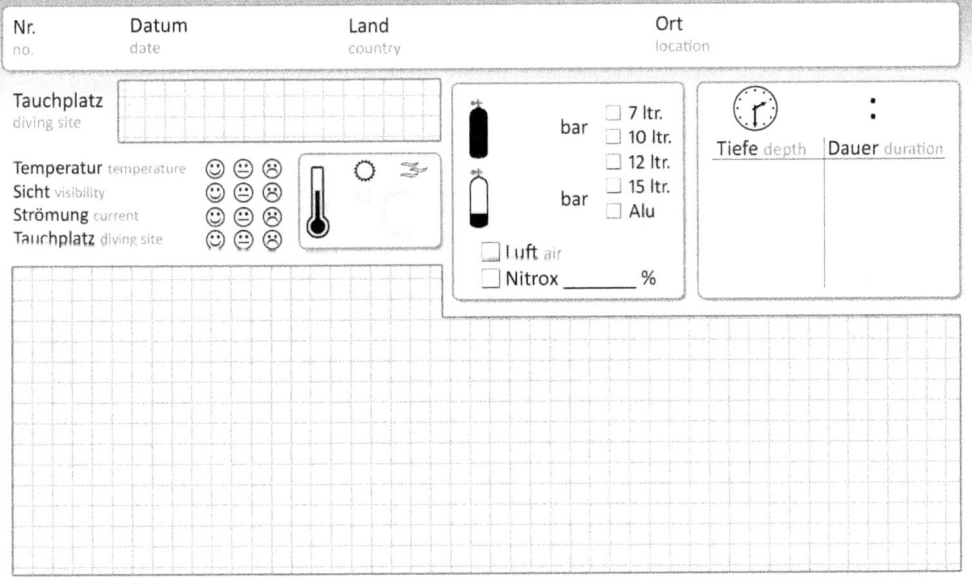

Nr. no.	Datum date	Land country		Ort location	

Tauchplatz diving site

Temperatur temperature ☺ 😐 ☹
Sicht visibility ☺ 😐 ☹
Strömung current ☺ 😐 ☹
Tauchplatz diving site ☺ 😐 ☹

bar
bar
☐ 7 ltr.
☐ 10 ltr.
☐ 12 ltr.
☐ 15 ltr.
☐ Alu
☐ Luft air
☐ Nitrox _____ %

Tiefe depth | Dauer duration

Instructor
Signature:

Buddies

No.:

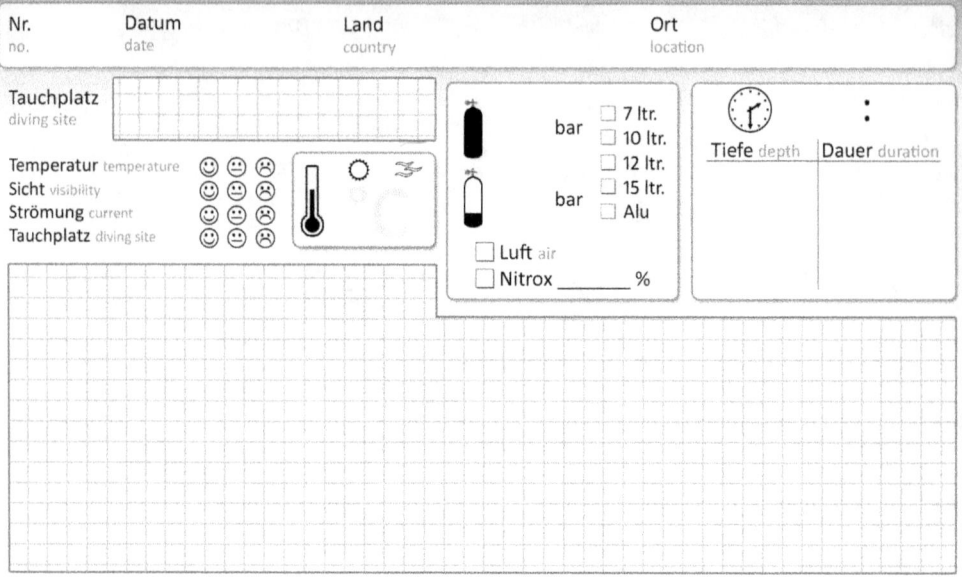

Instructor Buddies
Signature:

No.:

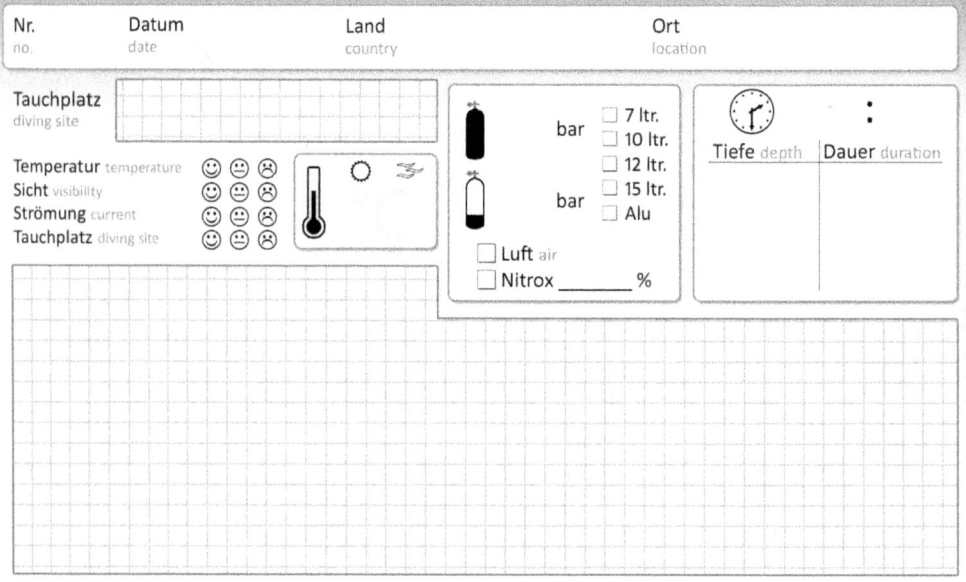

Instructor Buddies
Signature:

No.:

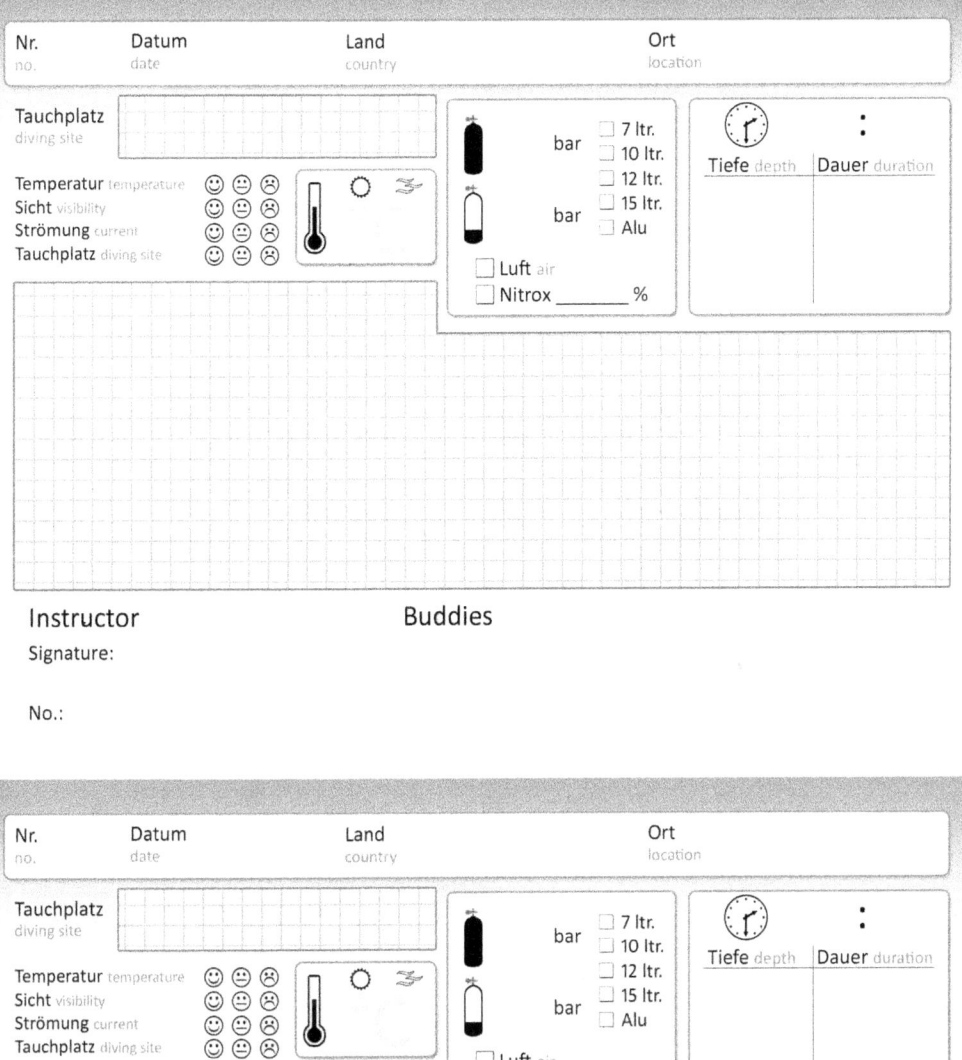

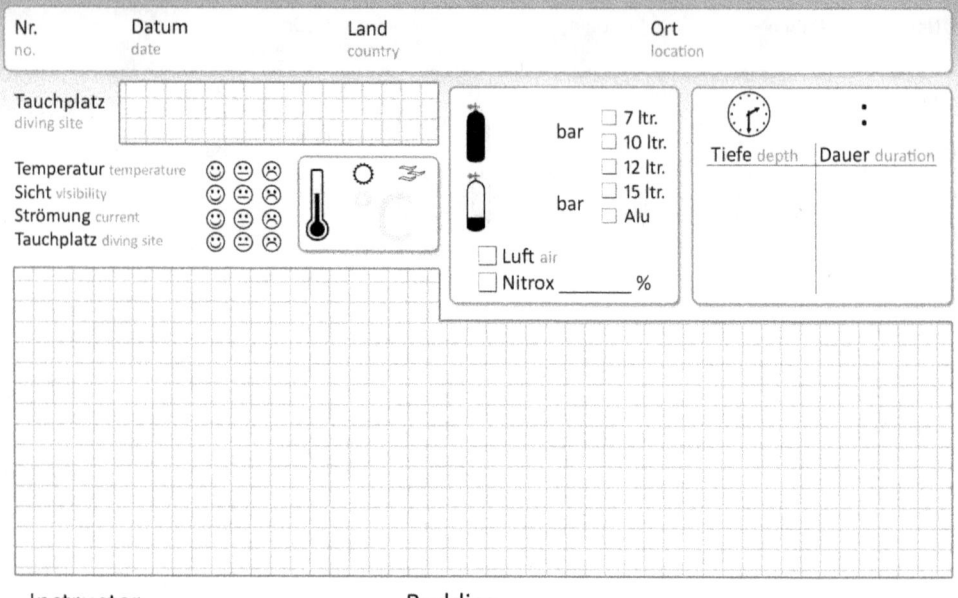

Instructor   Buddies

Signature:

No.:

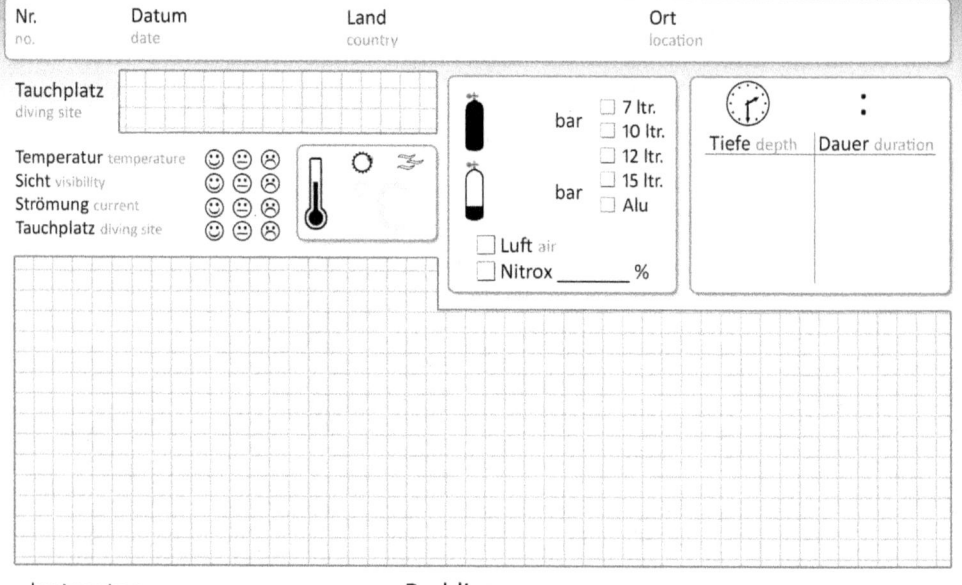

Instructor   Buddies

Signature:

No.:

Nr. no. | Datum date | Land country | Ort location

Tauchplatz diving site

Temperatur temperature ☺ 😐 ☹
Sicht visibility ☺ 😐 ☹
Strömung current ☺ 😐 ☹
Tauchplatz diving site ☺ 😐 ☹

bar
bar

☐ 7 ltr.
☐ 10 ltr.
☐ 12 ltr.
☐ 15 ltr.
☐ Alu

☐ Luft air
☐ Nitrox ________ %

:

Tiefe depth | Dauer duration

Instructor

Signature:

No.:

Buddies

Nr. no. | Datum date | Land country | Ort location

Tauchplatz diving site

Temperatur temperature ☺ 😐 ☹
Sicht visibility ☺ 😐 ☹
Strömung current ☺ 😐 ☹
Tauchplatz diving site ☺ 😐 ☹

bar
bar

☐ 7 ltr.
☐ 10 ltr.
☐ 12 ltr.
☐ 15 ltr.
☐ Alu

☐ Luft air
☐ Nitrox ________ %

:

Tiefe depth | Dauer duration

Instructor

Signature:

No.:

Buddies

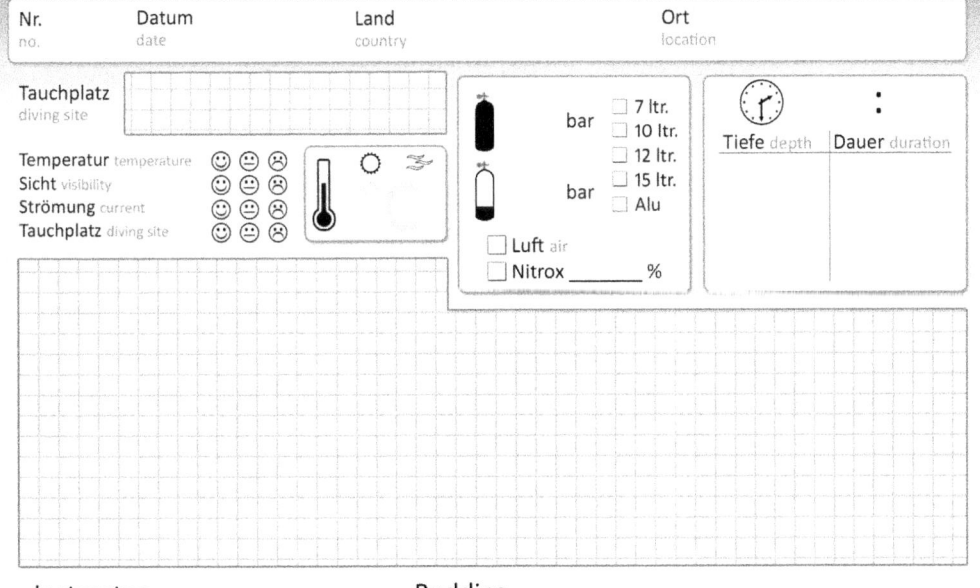

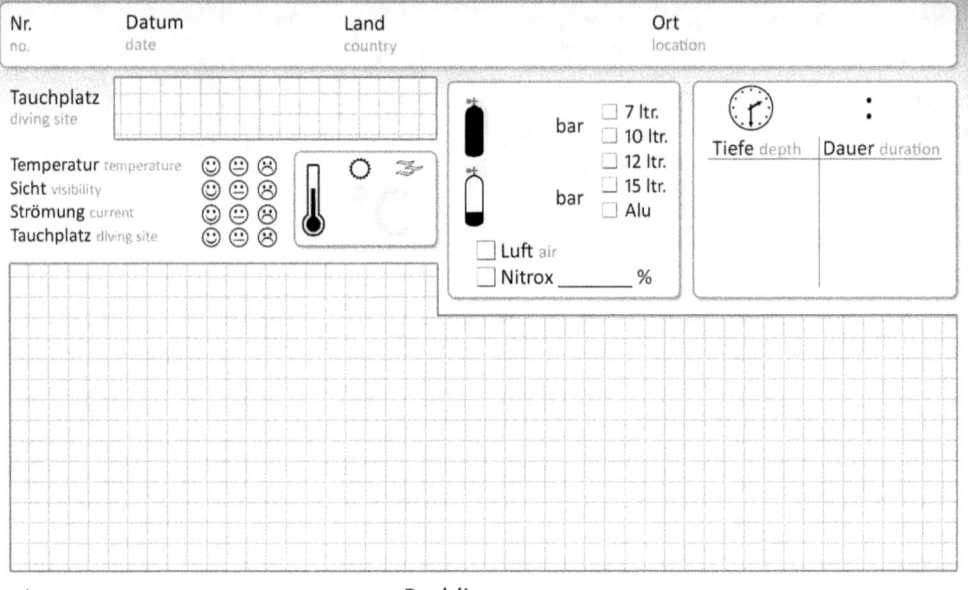

Instructor   Buddies

Signature:

No.:

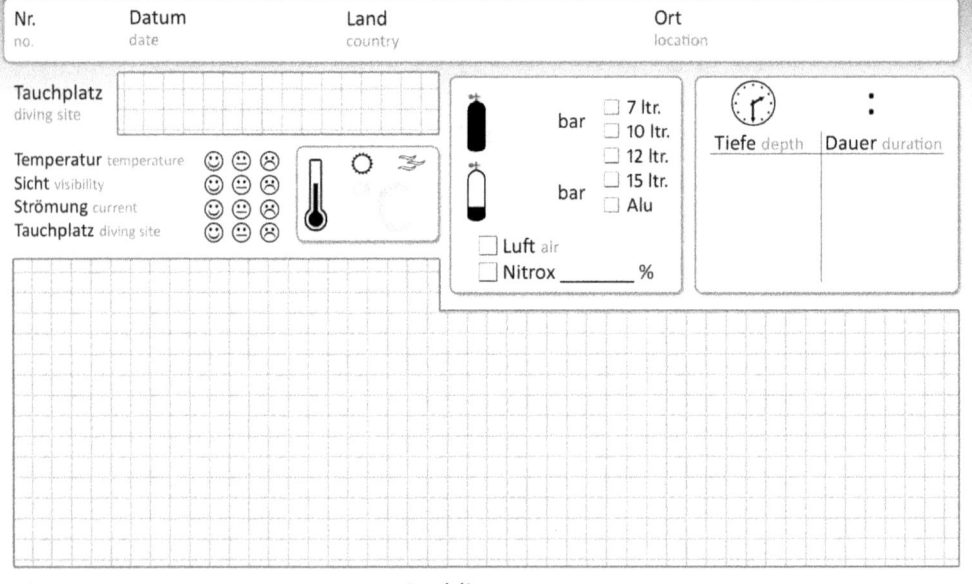

Instructor   Buddies

Signature:

No.:

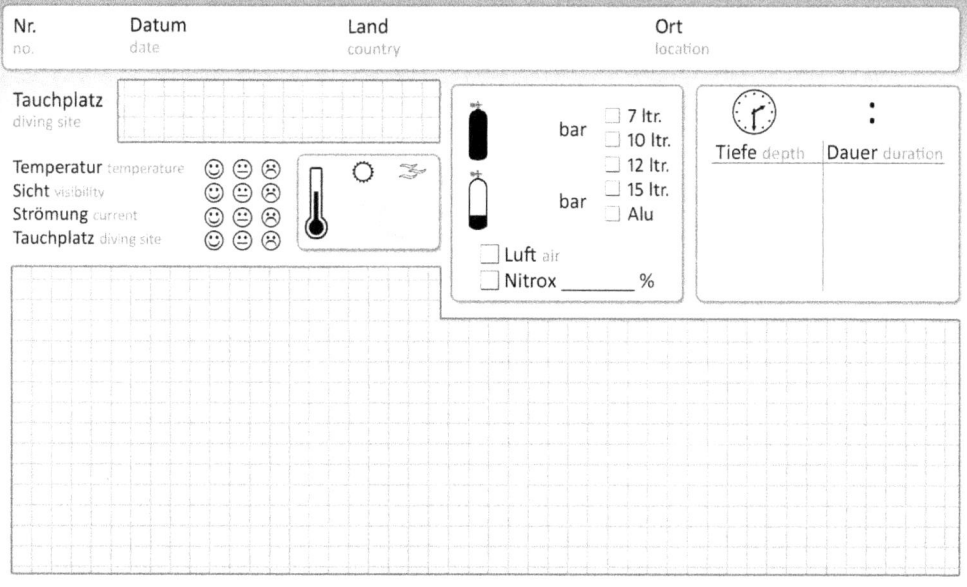

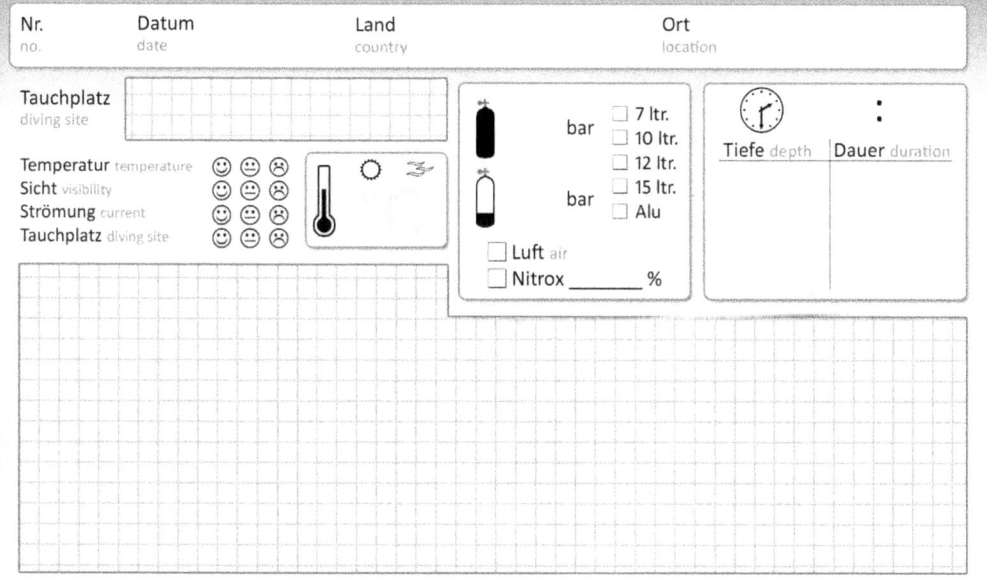

Nr. no.	Datum date	Land country	Ort location

Tauchplatz diving site

Temperatur temperature ☺ 😐 ☹
Sicht visibility ☺ 😐 ☹
Strömung current ☺ 😐 ☹
Tauchplatz diving site ☺ 😐 ☹

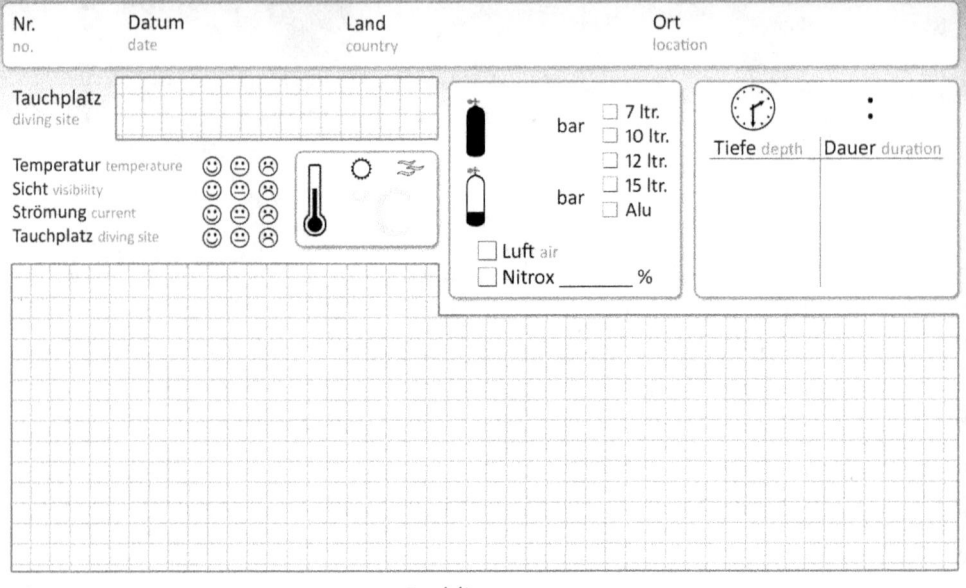

bar
☐ 7 ltr.
☐ 10 ltr.
☐ 12 ltr.
☐ 15 ltr.
☐ Alu
bar

☐ Luft air
☐ Nitrox _____ %

Tiefe depth | **Dauer** duration

Instructor
Signature:

Buddies

No.:

Nr. no.	Datum date	Land country	Ort location

Tauchplatz diving site

Temperatur temperature ☺ 😐 ☹
Sicht visibility ☺ 😐 ☹
Strömung current ☺ 😐 ☹
Tauchplatz diving site ☺ 😐 ☹

bar
☐ 7 ltr.
☐ 10 ltr.
☐ 12 ltr.
☐ 15 ltr.
☐ Alu
bar

☐ Luft air
☐ Nitrox _____ %

Tiefe depth | **Dauer** duration

Instructor
Signature:

Buddies

No.:

Nr. no.	Datum date	Land country		Ort location	

Tauchplatz diving site

Temperatur temperature ☺ ☺ ☹
Sicht visibility ☺ ☺ ☹
Strömung current ☺ ☺ ☹
Tauchplatz diving site ☺ ☺ ☹

bar
☐ 7 ltr.
☐ 10 ltr.
☐ 12 ltr.
bar ☐ 15 ltr.
☐ Alu
☐ Luft air
☐ Nitrox ____ %

Tiefe depth	Dauer duration

Instructor   **Buddies**
Signature:

No.:

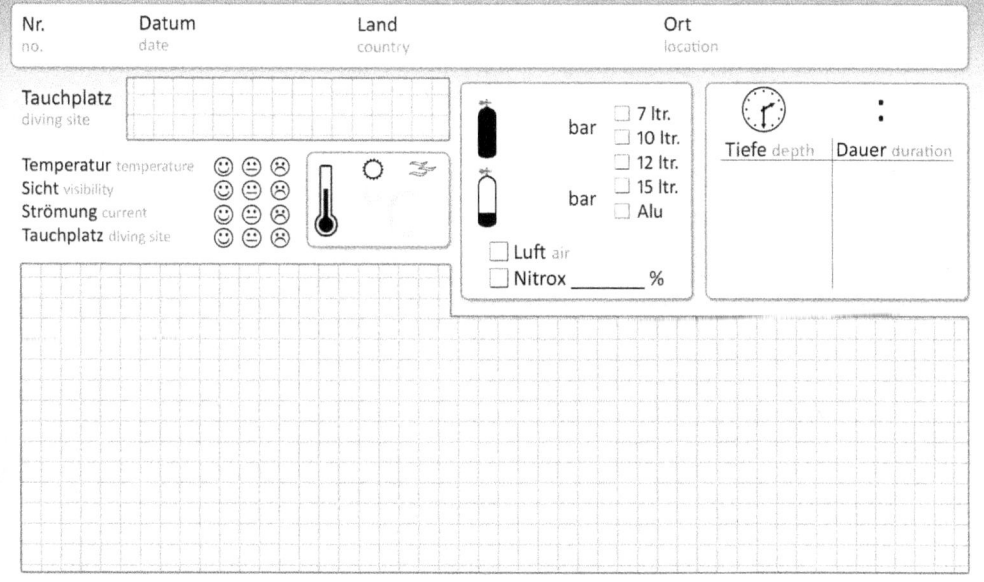

Nr. no.	Datum date	Land country		Ort location	

Tauchplatz diving site

Temperatur temperature ☺ ☺ ☹
Sicht visibility ☺ ☺ ☹
Strömung current ☺ ☺ ☹
Tauchplatz diving site ☺ ☺ ☹

bar
☐ 7 ltr.
☐ 10 ltr.
☐ 12 ltr.
bar ☐ 15 ltr.
☐ Alu
☐ Luft air
☐ Nitrox ____ %

Tiefe depth	Dauer duration

Instructor   **Buddies**
Signature:

No.:

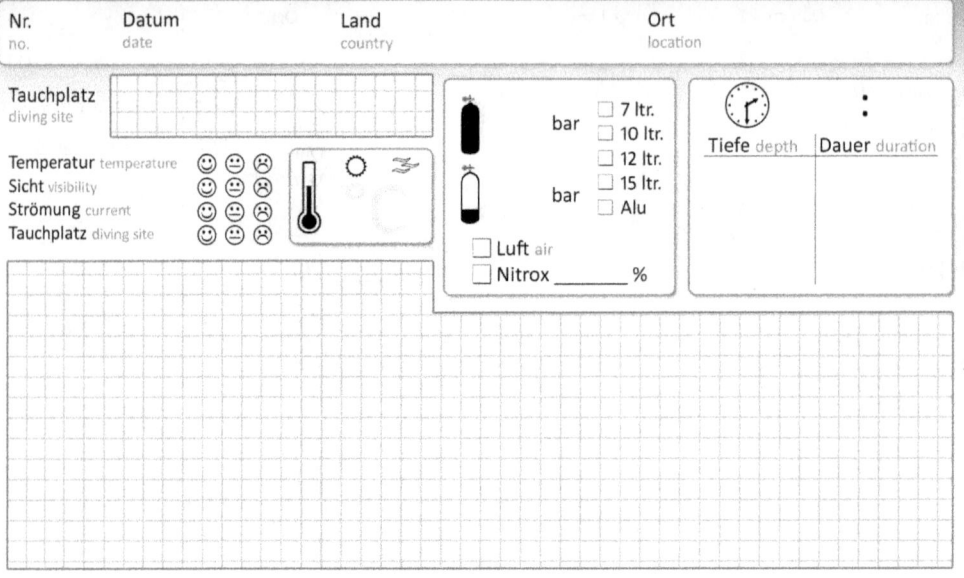

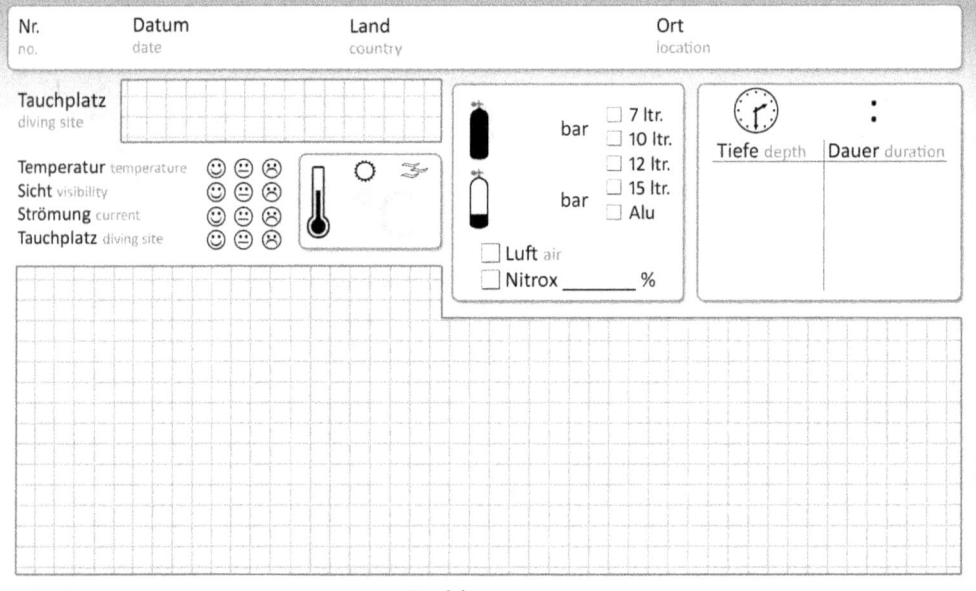

| Nr. no. | Datum date | Land country | Ort location |

Tauchplatz diving site

Temperatur temperature ☺ 😐 ☹
Sicht visibility ☺ 😐 ☹
Strömung current ☺ 😐 ☹
Tauchplatz diving site ☺ 😐 ☹

bar ☐ 7 ltr. ☐ 10 ltr. ☐ 12 ltr.
bar ☐ 15 ltr. ☐ Alu
☐ Luft air
☐ Nitrox _____ %

Tiefe depth | **Dauer** duration

Instructor   Buddies
Signature:

No.:

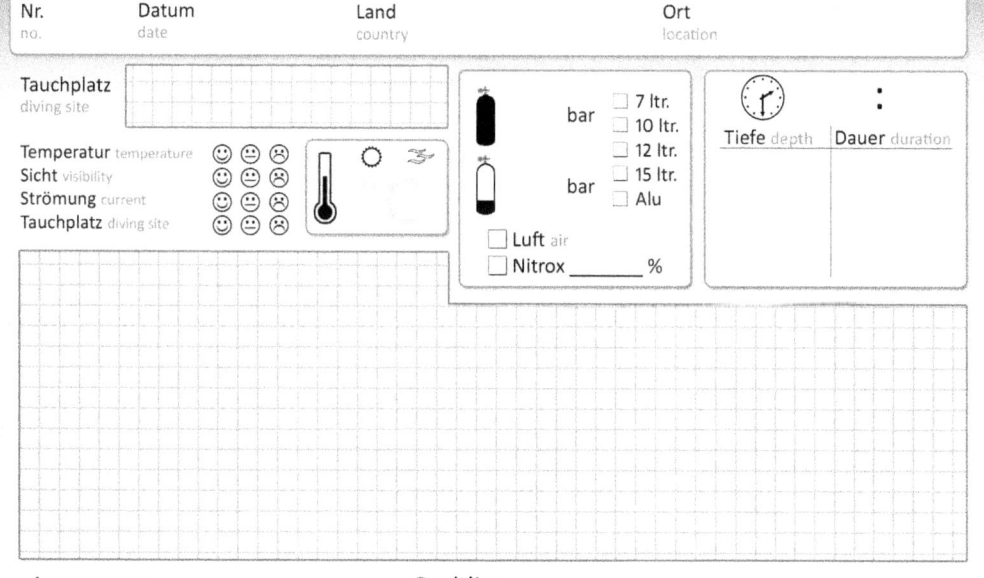

| Nr. no. | Datum date | Land country | Ort location |

Tauchplatz diving site

Temperatur temperature ☺ 😐 ☹
Sicht visibility ☺ 😐 ☹
Strömung current ☺ 😐 ☹
Tauchplatz diving site ☺ 😐 ☹

bar ☐ 7 ltr. ☐ 10 ltr. ☐ 12 ltr.
bar ☐ 15 ltr. ☐ Alu
☐ Luft air
☐ Nitrox _____ %

Tiefe depth | **Dauer** duration

Instructor   Buddies
Signature:

No.:

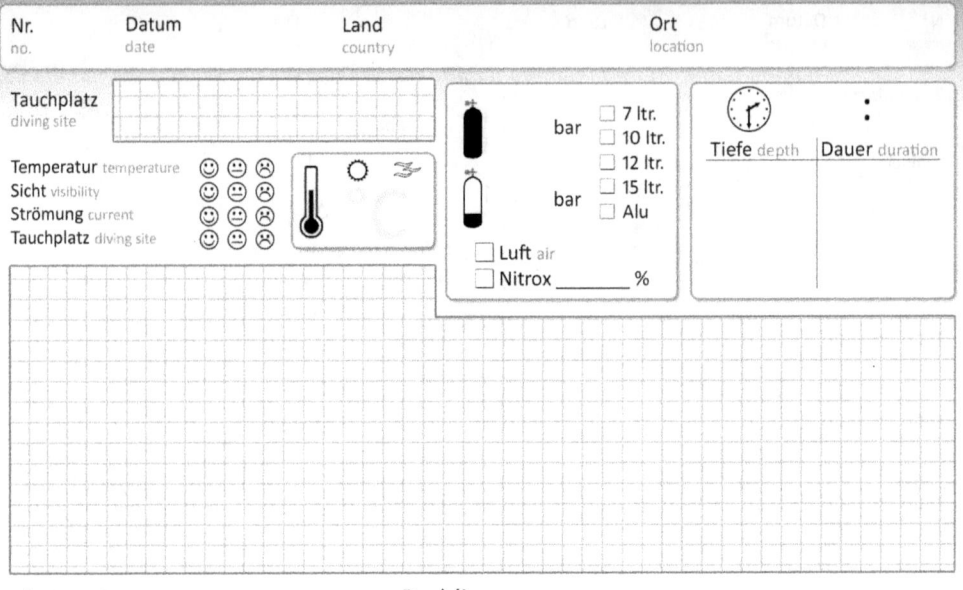

Instructor   Buddies
Signature:

No.:

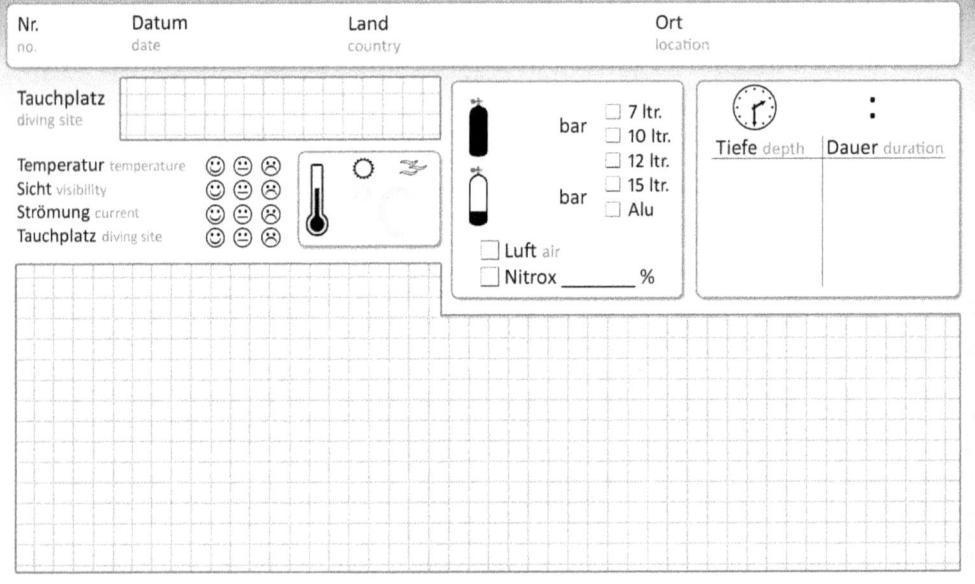

Instructor   Buddies
Signature:

No.:

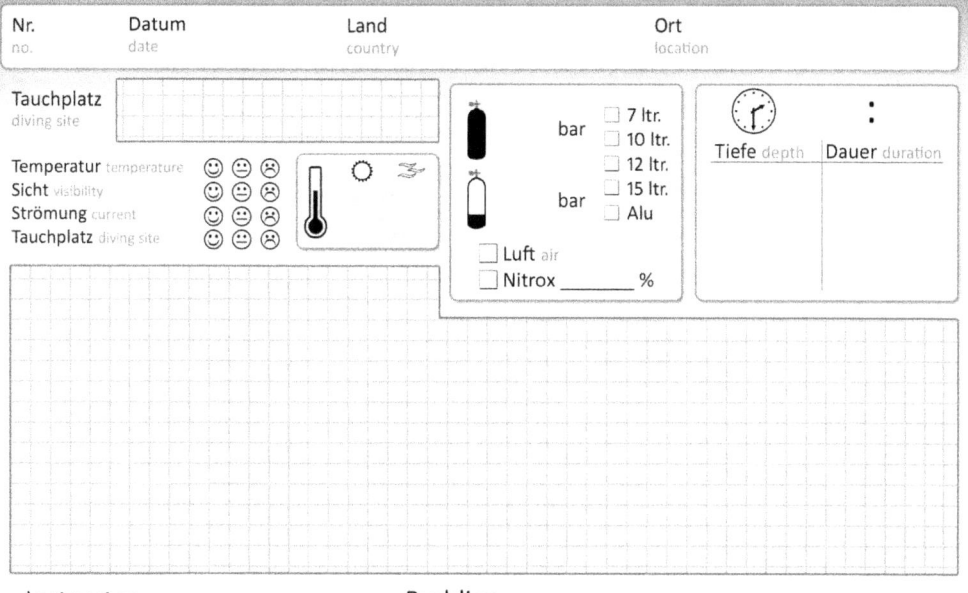

Instructor   Buddies
Signature:

No.:

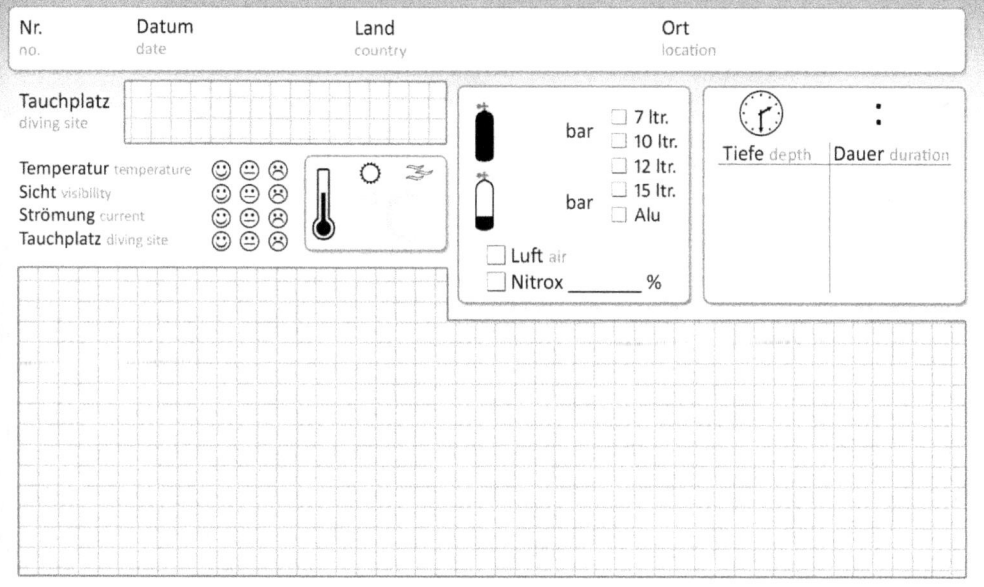

Instructor   Buddies
Signature:

No.:

Nr. no.	Datum date	Land country		Ort location	

Tauchplatz diving site

Temperatur temperature ☺ ☹ ☹
Sicht visibility ☺ ☹ ☹
Strömung current ☺ ☹ ☹
Tauchplatz diving site ☺ ☹ ☹

☐ 7 ltr.
☐ 10 ltr.
☐ 12 ltr.
☐ 15 ltr.
☐ Alu
☐ Luft air
☐ Nitrox _____ %

bar
bar

Tiefe depth	Dauer duration

Instructor
Signature:

Buddies

No.:

Nr. no.	Datum date	Land country		Ort location	

Tauchplatz diving site

Temperatur temperature ☺ ☹ ☹
Sicht visibility ☺ ☹ ☹
Strömung current ☺ ☹ ☹
Tauchplatz diving site ☺ ☹ ☹

☐ 7 ltr.
☐ 10 ltr.
☐ 12 ltr.
☐ 15 ltr.
☐ Alu
☐ Luft air
☐ Nitrox _____ %

bar
bar

Tiefe depth	Dauer duration

Instructor
Signature:

Buddies

No.:

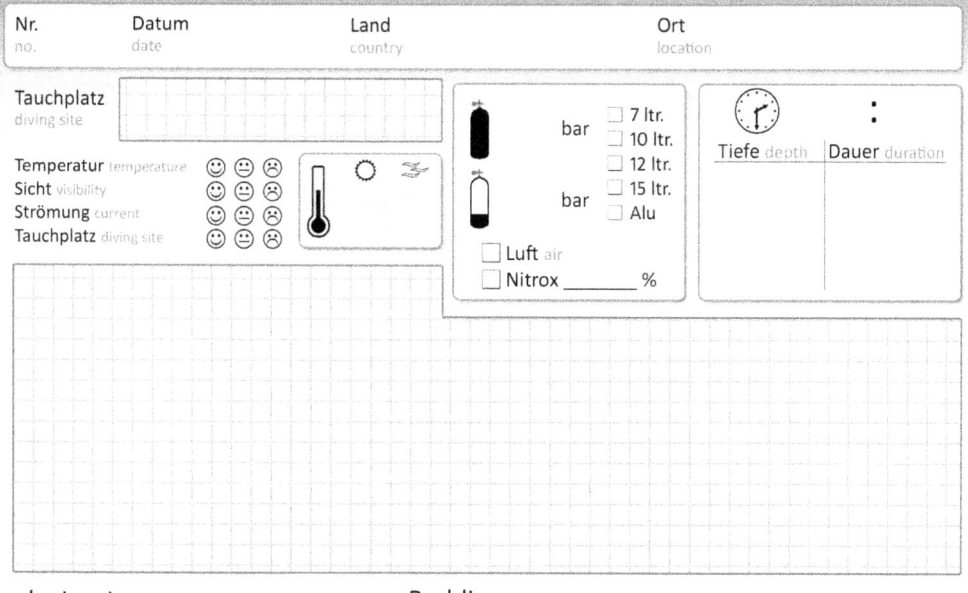

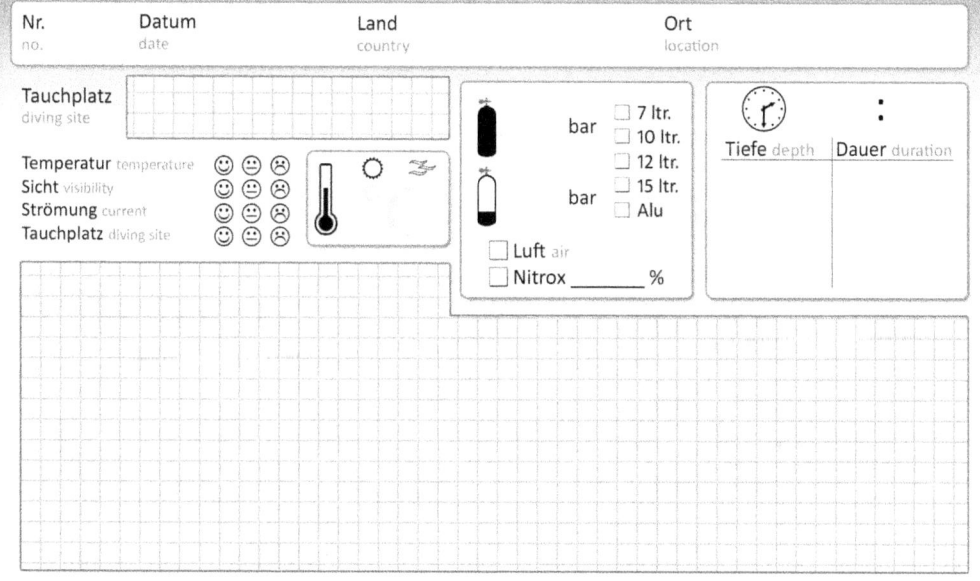

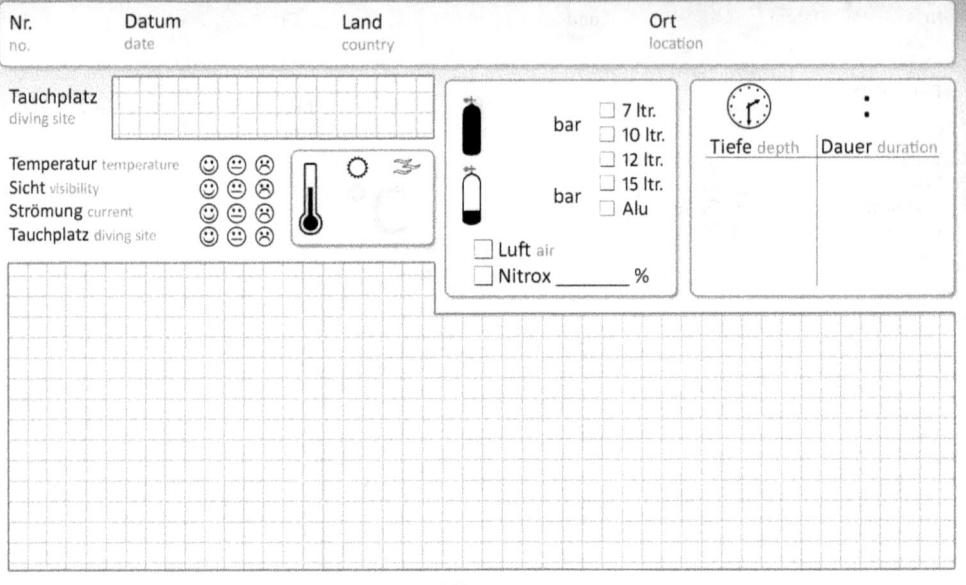

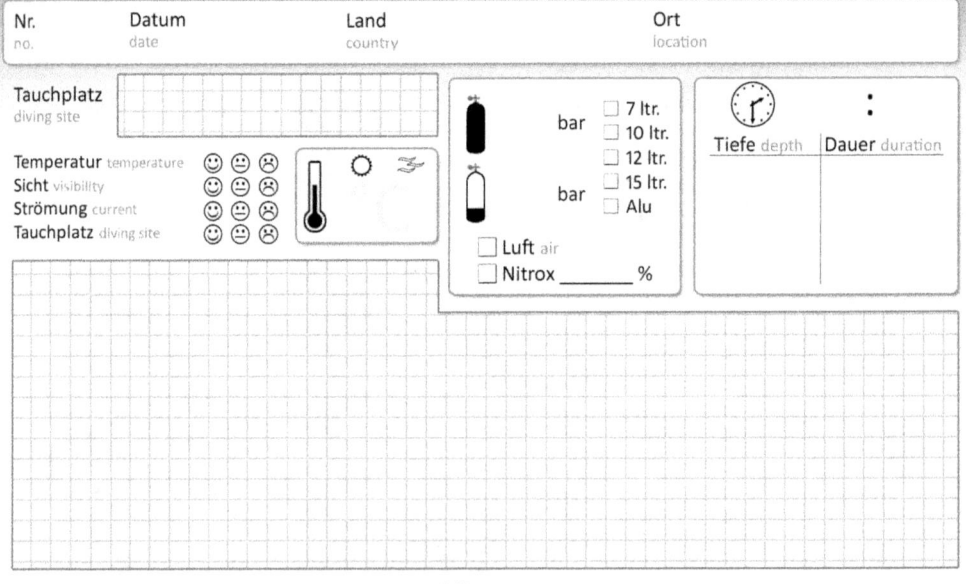

| Nr. no. | Datum date | Land country | Ort location |

Tauchplatz diving site

Temperatur temperature ☺ ☺ ☹
Sicht visibility ☺ ☺ ☹
Strömung current ☺ ☺ ☹
Tauchplatz diving site ☺ ☺ ☹

bar
☐ 7 ltr.
☐ 10 ltr.
☐ 12 ltr.
bar ☐ 15 ltr.
☐ Alu
☐ Luft air
☐ Nitrox _____ %

Tiefe depth | Dauer duration

Instructor   Buddies
Signature:

No.:

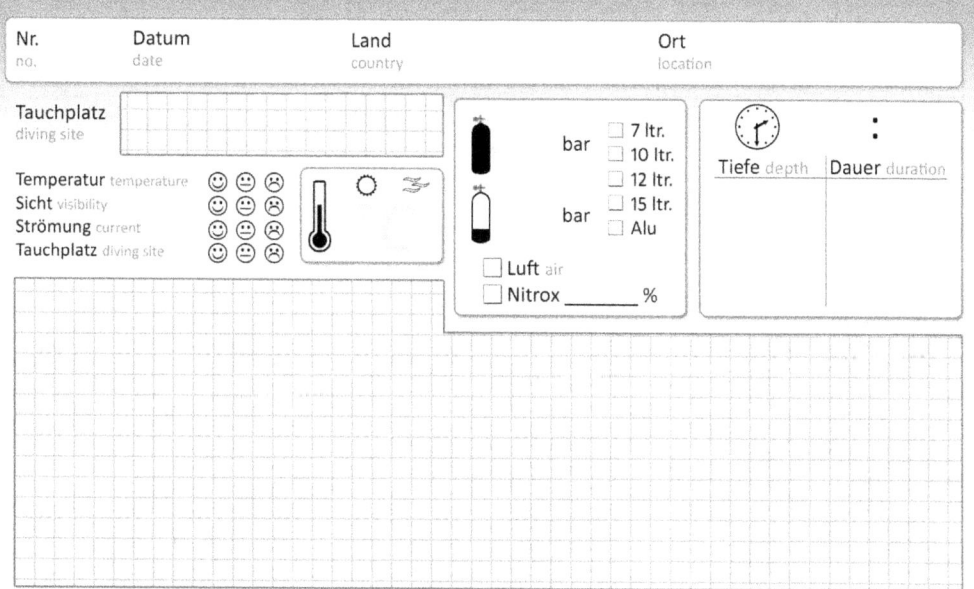

| Nr. no. | Datum date | Land country | Ort location |

Tauchplatz diving site

Temperatur temperature ☺ ☺ ☹
Sicht visibility ☺ ☺ ☹
Strömung current ☺ ☺ ☹
Tauchplatz diving site ☺ ☺ ☹

bar
☐ 7 ltr.
☐ 10 ltr.
☐ 12 ltr.
bar ☐ 15 ltr.
☐ Alu
☐ Luft air
☐ Nitrox _____ %

Tiefe depth | Dauer duration

Instructor   Buddies
Signature:

No.:

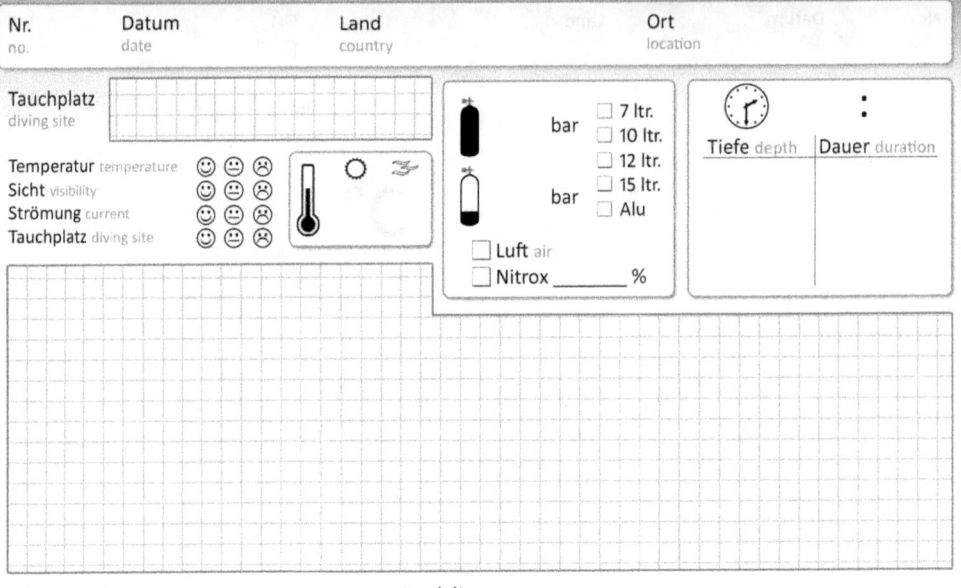

Instructor   Buddies

Signature:

No.:

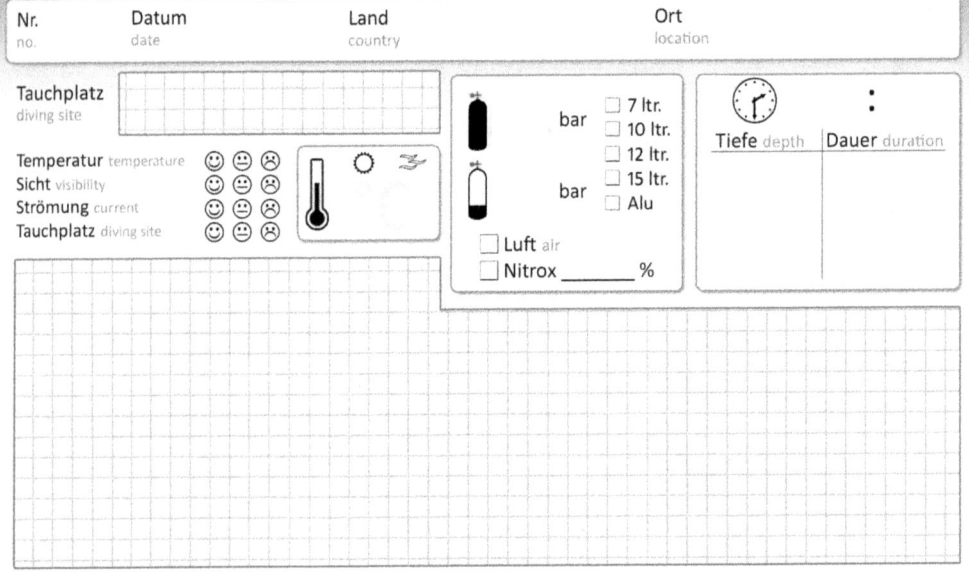

Instructor   Buddies

Signature:

No.:

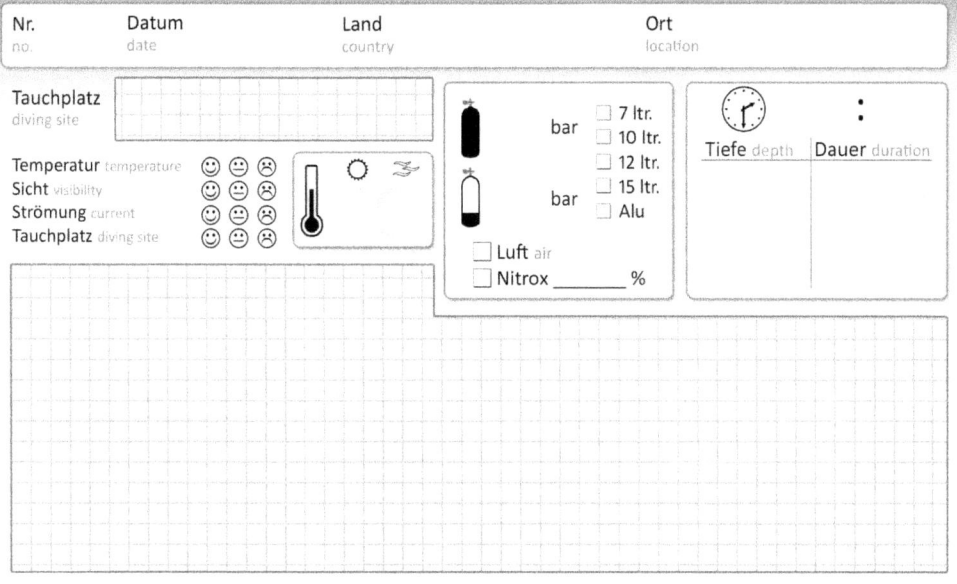

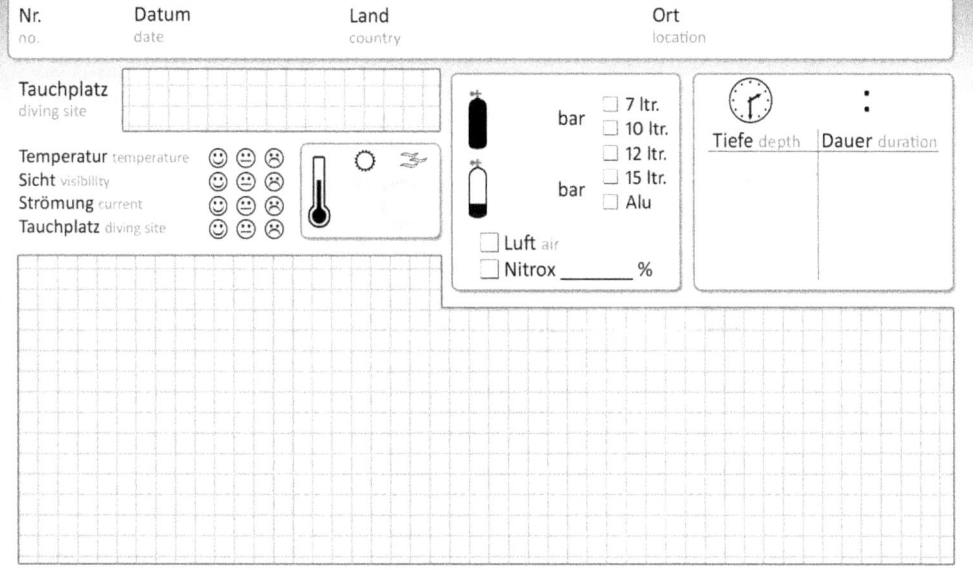

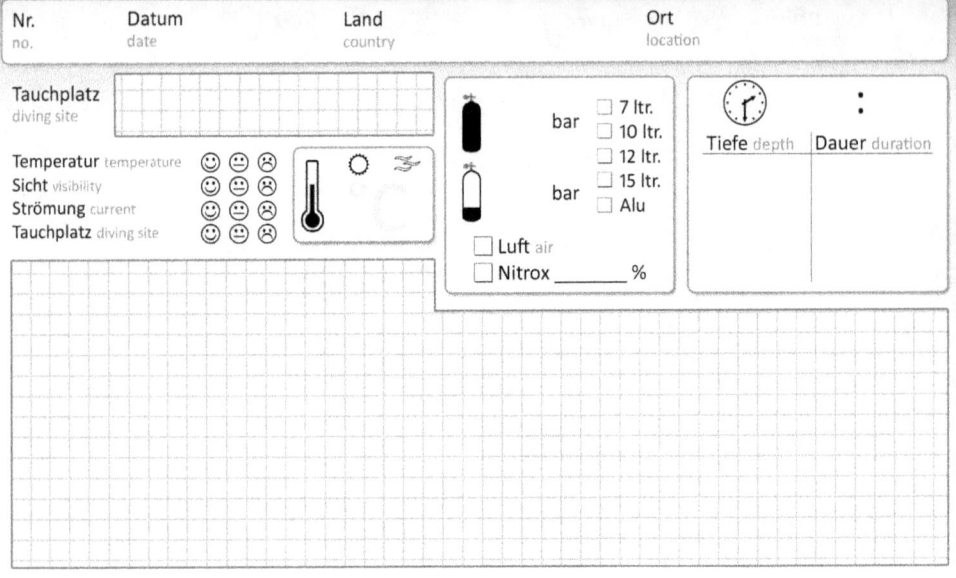

Instructor   Buddies

Signature:

No.:

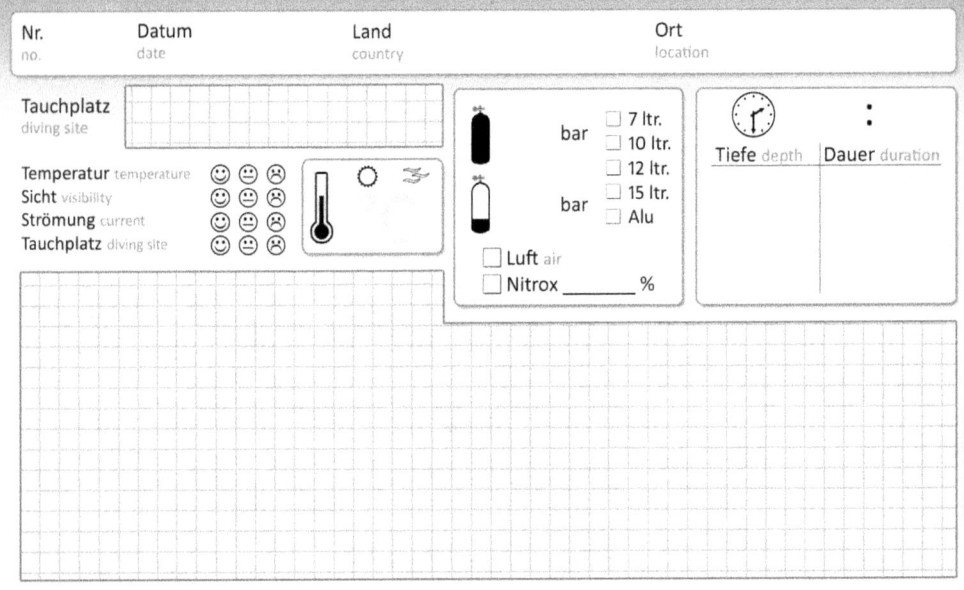

Instructor   Buddies

Signature:

No.:

Nr. no.	Datum date	Land country	Ort location

Tauchplatz diving site

Temperatur temperature ☺ 😐 ☹
Sicht visibility ☺ 😐 ☹
Strömung current ☺ 😐 ☹
Tauchplatz diving site ☺ 😐 ☹

bar ☐ 7 ltr. ☐ 10 ltr. ☐ 12 ltr.
bar ☐ 15 ltr. ☐ Alu
☐ Luft air
☐ Nitrox _____ %

Tiefe depth | **Dauer** duration

Instructor   **Buddies**

Signature:

No.:

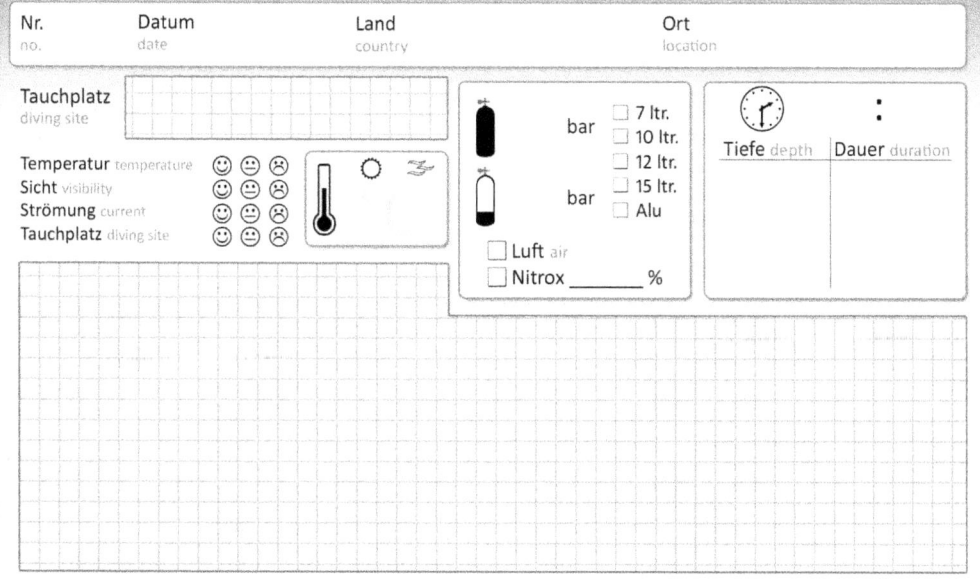

Nr. no.	Datum date	Land country	Ort location

Tauchplatz diving site

Temperatur temperature ☺ 😐 ☹
Sicht visibility ☺ 😐 ☹
Strömung current ☺ 😐 ☹
Tauchplatz diving site ☺ 😐 ☹

bar ☐ 7 ltr. ☐ 10 ltr. ☐ 12 ltr.
bar ☐ 15 ltr. ☐ Alu
☐ Luft air
☐ Nitrox _____ %

Tiefe depth | **Dauer** duration

Instructor   **Buddies**

Signature:

No.:

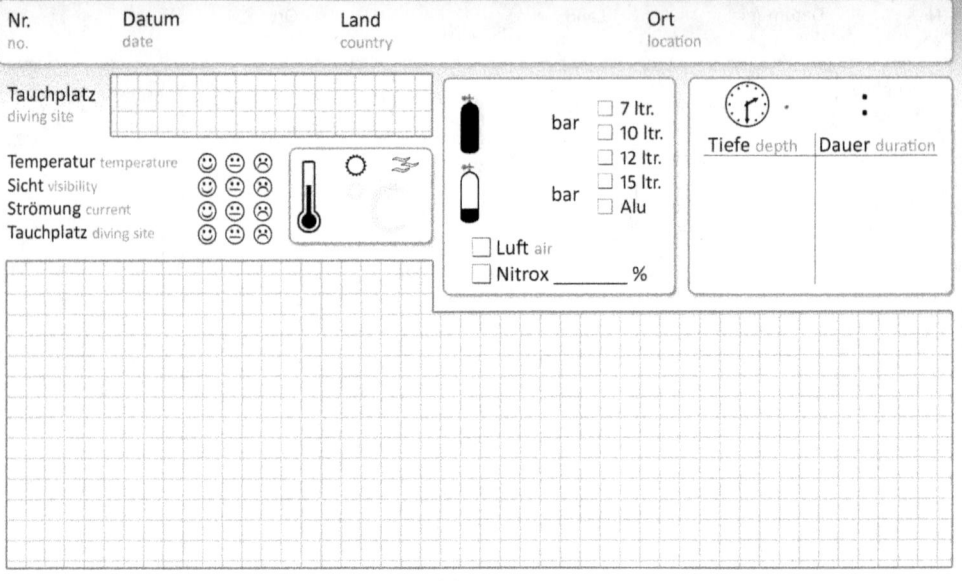

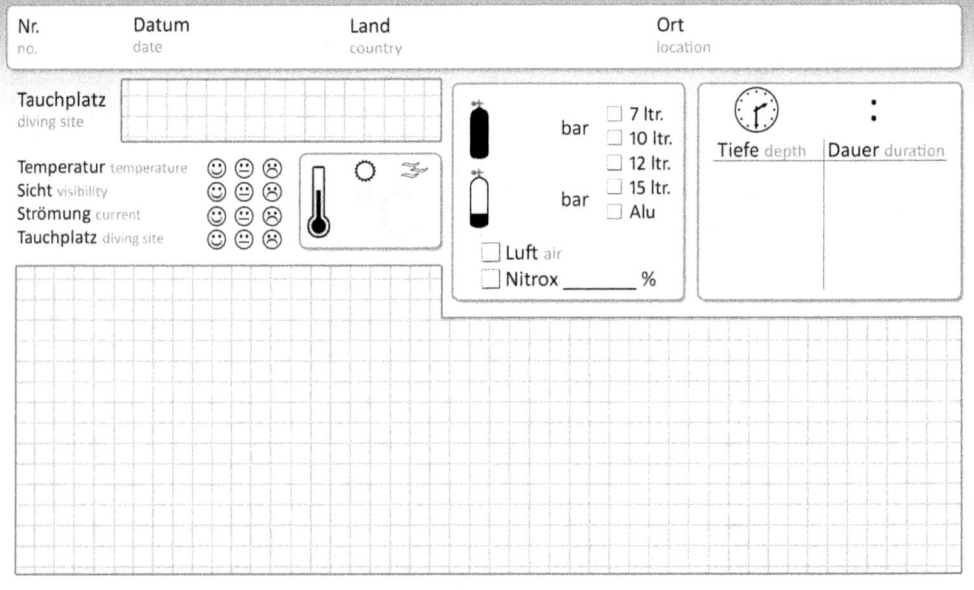

Nr. no. | Datum date | Land country | Ort location

Tauchplatz diving site

Temperatur temperature ☺ 😐 ☹
Sicht visibility ☺ 😐 ☹
Strömung current ☺ 😐 ☹
Tauchplatz diving site ☺ 😐 ☹

bar
bar

☐ 7 ltr.
☐ 10 ltr.
☐ 12 ltr.
☐ 15 ltr.
☐ Alu

☐ Luft air
☐ Nitrox ________ %

:

Tiefe depth	Dauer duration

Instructor

Signature:

No.:

Buddies

Nr. no. | Datum date | Land country | Ort location

Tauchplatz diving site

Temperatur temperature ☺ 😐 ☹
Sicht visibility ☺ 😐 ☹
Strömung current ☺ 😐 ☹
Tauchplatz diving site ☺ 😐 ☹

bar
bar

☐ 7 ltr.
☐ 10 ltr.
☐ 12 ltr.
☐ 15 ltr.
☐ Alu

☐ Luft air
☐ Nitrox ________ %

:

Tiefe depth	Dauer duration

Instructor

Signature:

No.:

Buddies

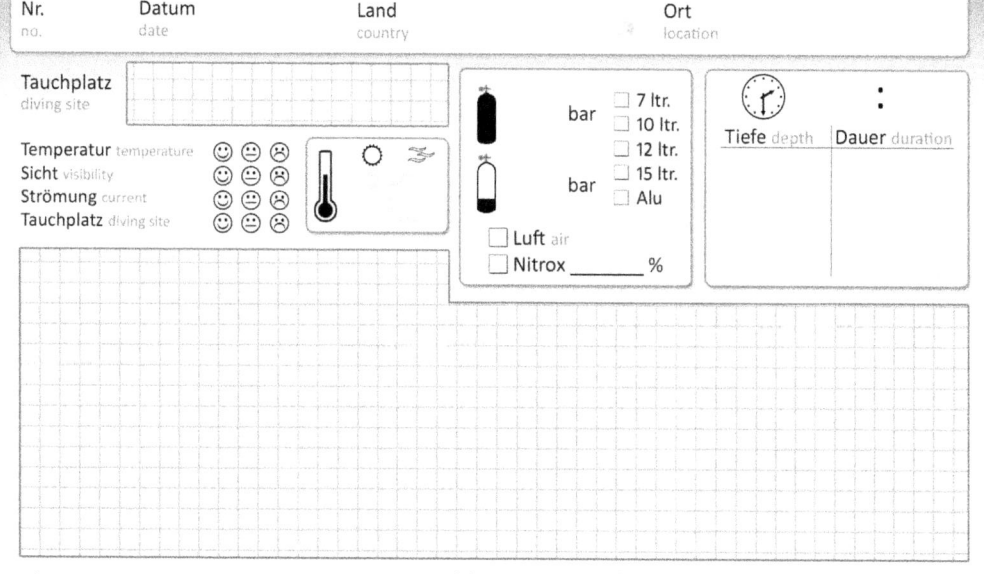

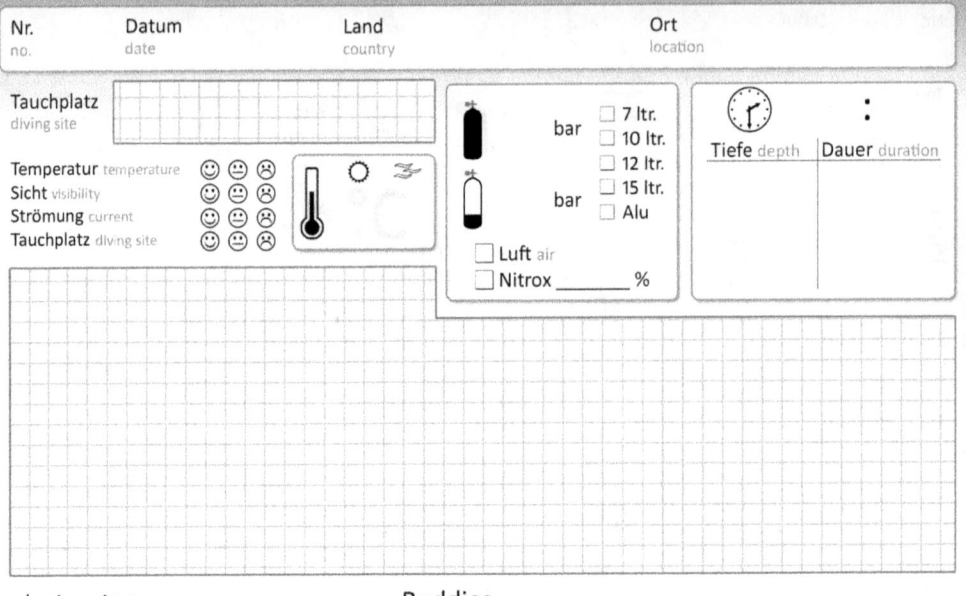

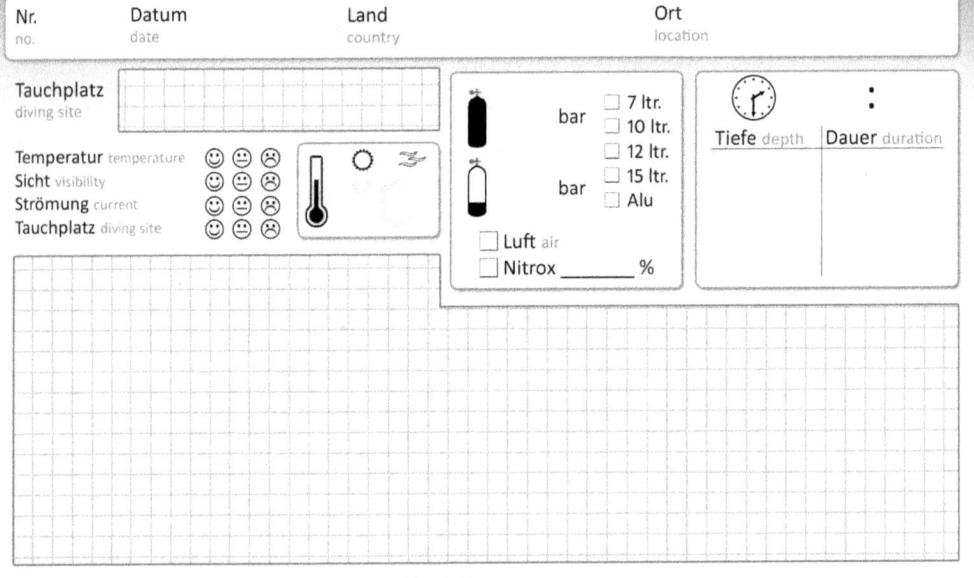

Nr. no.	Datum date	Land country		Ort location	

Tauchplatz diving site

Temperatur temperature ☺ 😐 ☹
Sicht visibility ☺ 😐 ☹
Strömung current ☺ 😐 ☹
Tauchplatz diving site ☺ 😐 ☹

☐ 7 ltr.
☐ 10 ltr.
bar ☐ 12 ltr.
☐ 15 ltr.
bar ☐ Alu

☐ Luft air
☐ Nitrox _____ %

Tiefe depth | Dauer duration

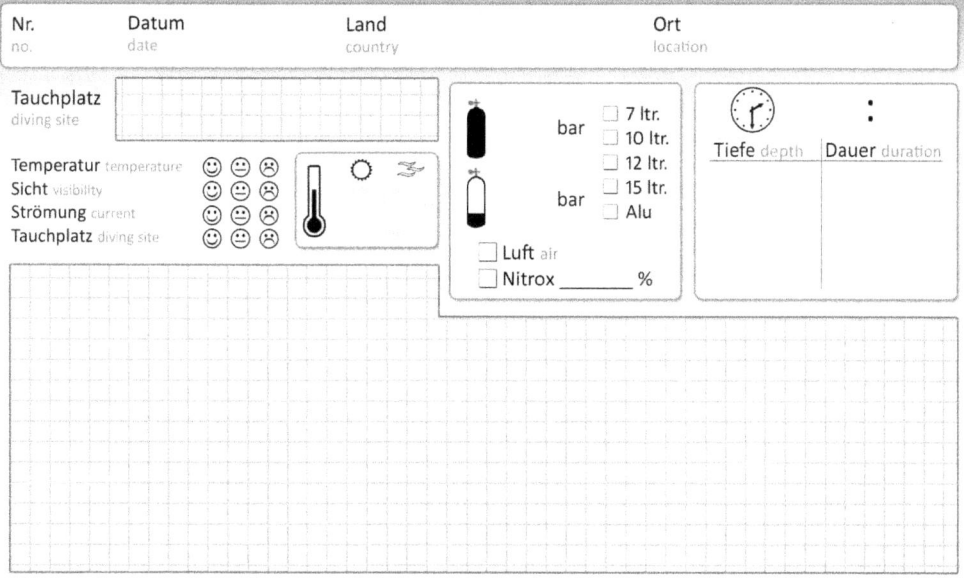

Instructor   **Buddies**
Signature:

No.:

Nr. no.	Datum date	Land country		Ort location	

Tauchplatz diving site

Temperatur temperature ☺ 😐 ☹
Sicht visibility ☺ 😐 ☹
Strömung current ☺ 😐 ☹
Tauchplatz diving site ☺ 😐 ☹

☐ 7 ltr.
☐ 10 ltr.
bar ☐ 12 ltr.
☐ 15 ltr.
bar ☐ Alu

☐ Luft air
☐ Nitrox _____ %

Tiefe depth | Dauer duration

Instructor   **Buddies**
Signature:

No.:

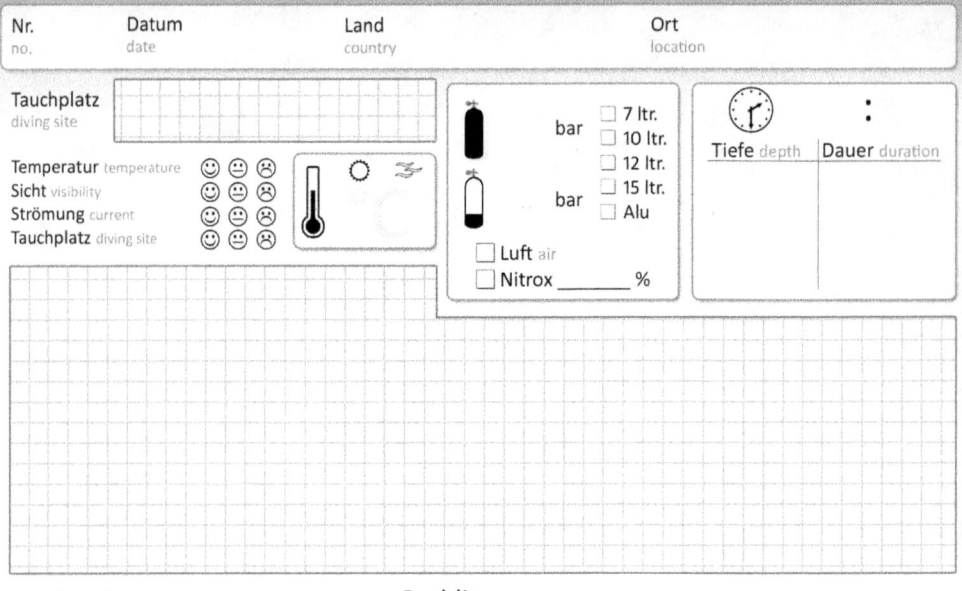

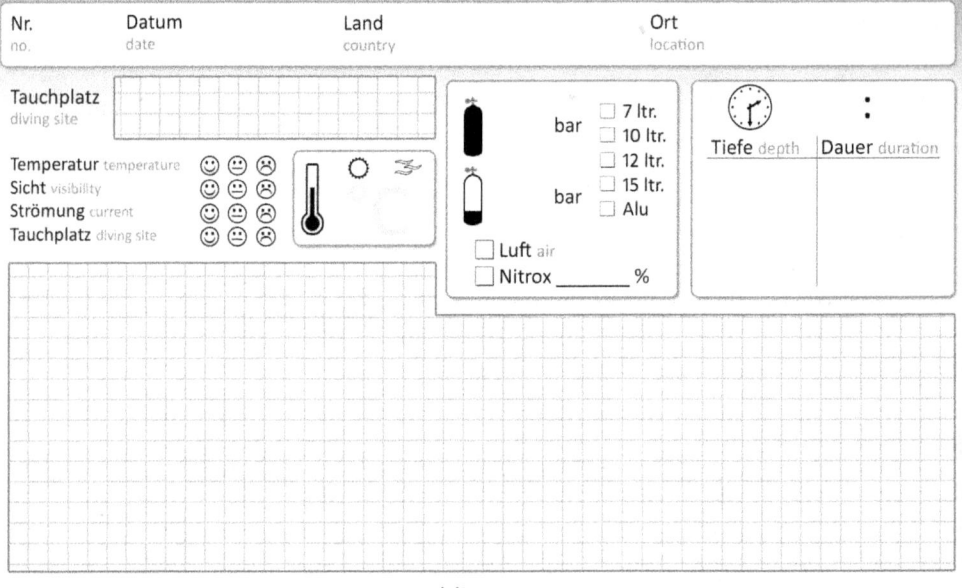

Nr. no.	Datum date	Land country		Ort location	

Tauchplatz diving site

Temperatur temperature ☺ 😐 ☹
Sicht visibility ☺ 😐 ☹
Strömung current ☺ 😐 ☹
Tauchplatz diving site ☺ 😐 ☹

bar ☐ 7 ltr. ☐ 10 ltr. ☐ 12 ltr.
bar ☐ 15 ltr. ☐ Alu
☐ Luft air
☐ Nitrox _____ %

Tiefe depth	Dauer duration

Instructor   Buddies
Signature:

No.:

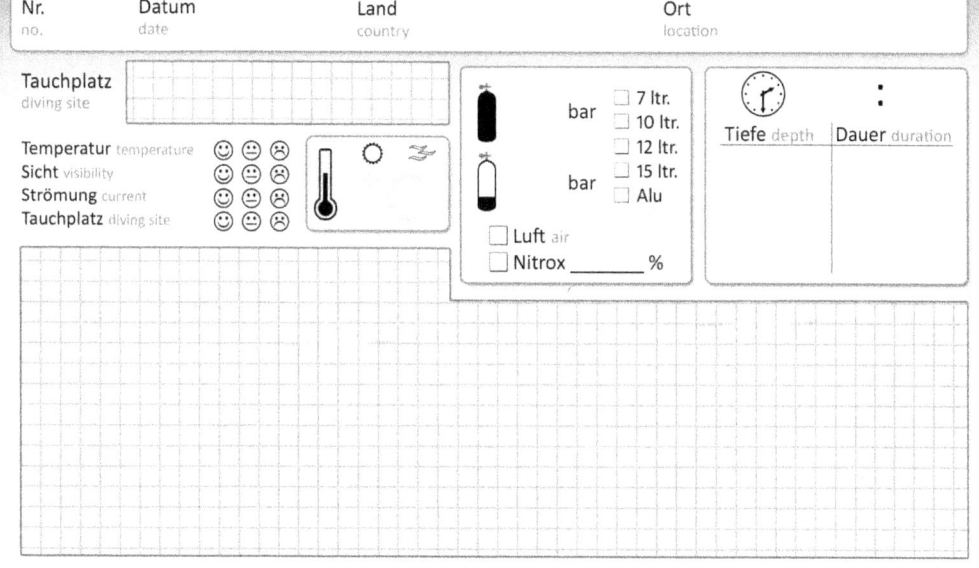

Nr. no.	Datum date	Land country		Ort location	

Tauchplatz diving site

Temperatur temperature ☺ 😐 ☹
Sicht visibility ☺ 😐 ☹
Strömung current ☺ 😐 ☹
Tauchplatz diving site ☺ 😐 ☹

bar ☐ 7 ltr. ☐ 10 ltr. ☐ 12 ltr.
bar ☐ 15 ltr. ☐ Alu
☐ Luft air
☐ Nitrox _____ %

Tiefe depth	Dauer duration

Instructor   Buddies
Signature:

No.:

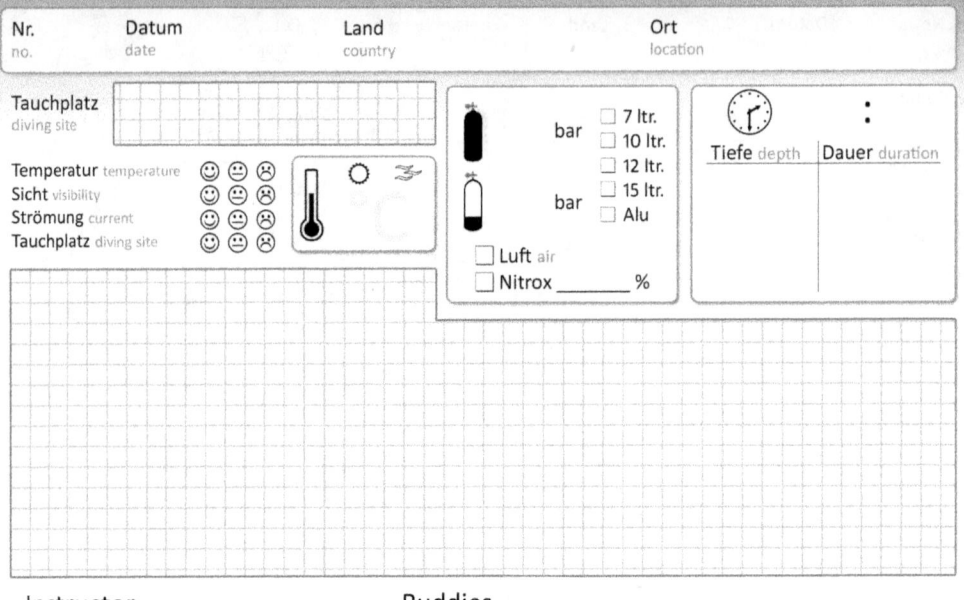

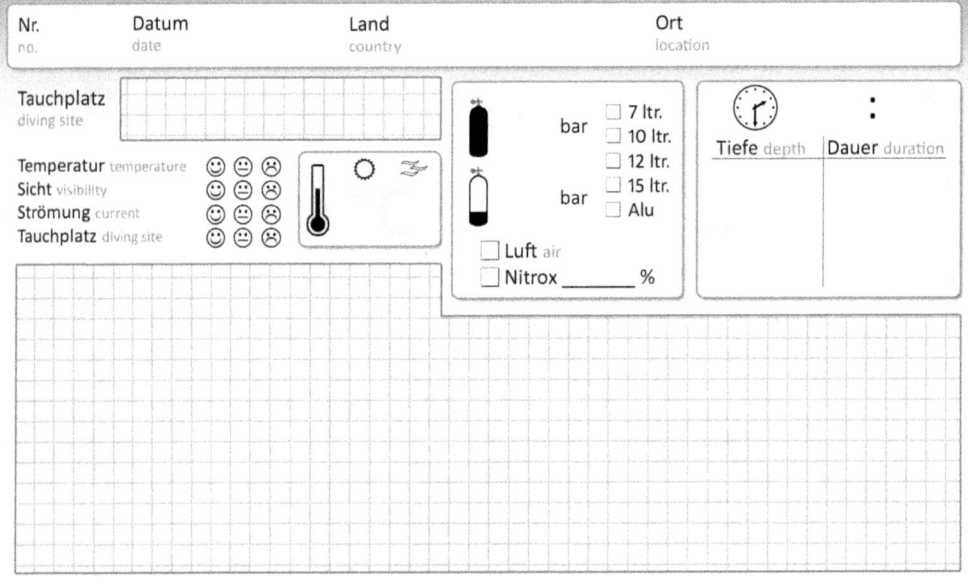

| Nr. no. | Datum date | Land country | Ort location |

Tauchplatz diving site

Temperatur temperature ☺ 😐 ☹
Sicht visibility ☺ 😐 ☹
Strömung current ☺ 😐 ☹
Tauchplatz diving site ☺ 😐 ☹

bar ☐ 7 ltr.
☐ 10 ltr.
☐ 12 ltr.
bar ☐ 15 ltr.
☐ Alu

☐ Luft air
☐ Nitrox _____ %

Tiefe depth | Dauer duration

Instructor   Buddies
Signature:

No.:

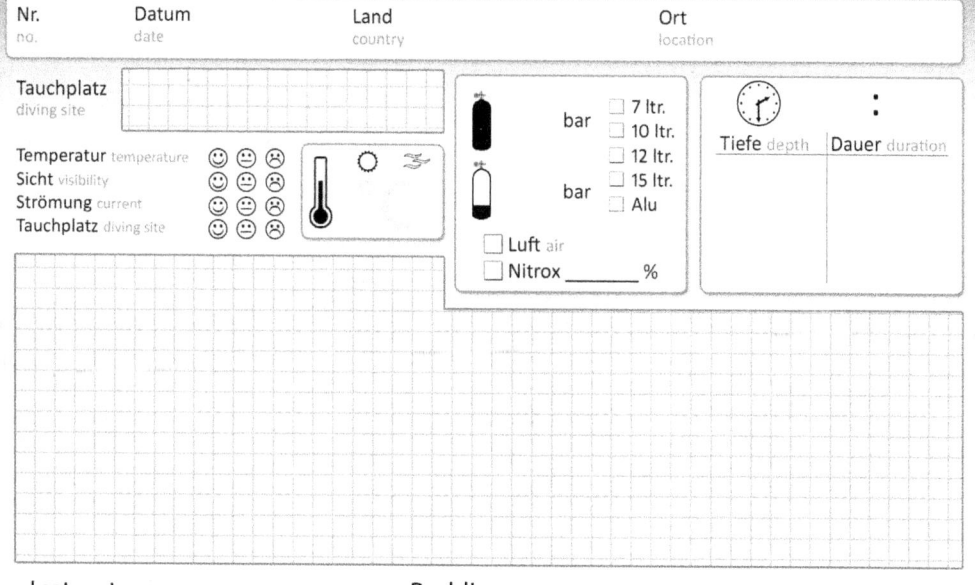

| Nr. no. | Datum date | Land country | Ort location |

Tauchplatz diving site

Temperatur temperature ☺ 😐 ☹
Sicht visibility ☺ 😐 ☹
Strömung current ☺ 😐 ☹
Tauchplatz diving site ☺ 😐 ☹

bar ☐ 7 ltr.
☐ 10 ltr.
☐ 12 ltr.
bar ☐ 15 ltr.
☐ Alu

☐ Luft air
☐ Nitrox _____ %

Tiefe depth | Dauer duration

Instructor   Buddies
Signature:

No.:

Nr. no. | Datum date | Land country | Ort location

Tauchplatz diving site

Temperatur temperature
Sicht visibility
Strömung current
Tauchplatz diving site

bar
bar

☐ 7 ltr.
☐ 10 ltr.
☐ 12 ltr.
☐ 15 ltr.
☐ Alu

☐ Luft air
☐ Nitrox _______ %

:

Tiefe depth	Dauer duration

Instructor

Buddies

Signature:

No.:

Nr. no. | Datum date | Land country | Ort location

Tauchplatz diving site

Temperatur temperature
Sicht visibility
Strömung current
Tauchplatz diving site

bar
bar

☐ 7 ltr.
☐ 10 ltr.
☐ 12 ltr.
☐ 15 ltr.
☐ Alu

☐ Luft air
☐ Nitrox _______ %

:

Tiefe depth	Dauer duration

Instructor

Buddies

Signature:

No.:

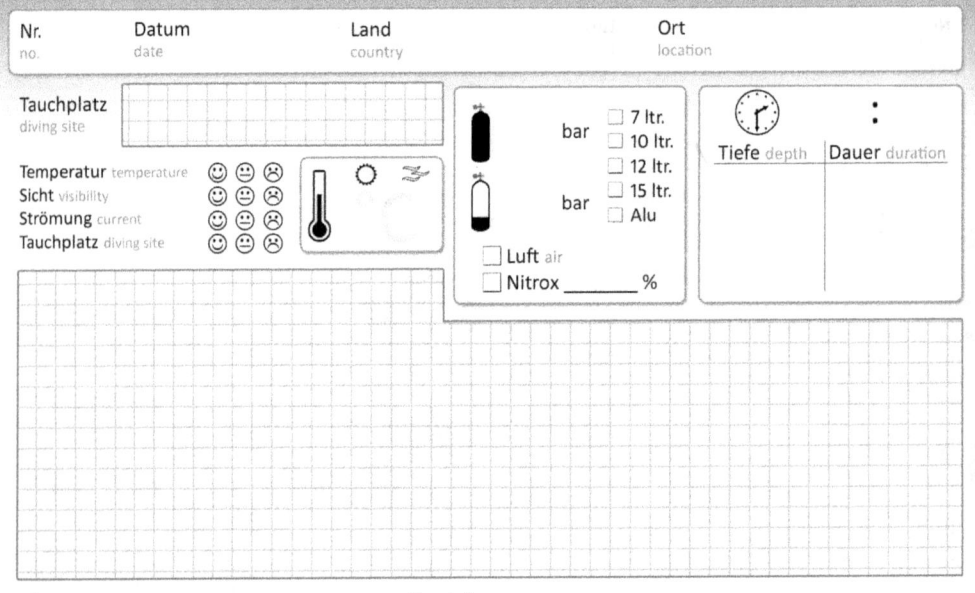

Nr. no.	Datum date	Land country		Ort location	

Tauchplatz diving site

Temperatur temperature ☺ 😐 ☹
Sicht visibility ☺ 😐 ☹
Strömung current ☺ 😐 ☹
Tauchplatz diving site ☺ 😐 ☹

bar ☐ 7 ltr.
☐ 10 ltr.
bar ☐ 12 ltr.
☐ 15 ltr.
☐ Alu

☐ Luft air
☐ Nitrox _____ %

Tiefe depth	Dauer duration

Instructor **Buddies**
Signature:

No.:

Nr. no.	Datum date	Land country		Ort location	

Tauchplatz diving site

Temperatur temperature ☺ 😐 ☹
Sicht visibility ☺ 😐 ☹
Strömung current ☺ 😐 ☹
Tauchplatz diving site ☺ 😐 ☹

bar ☐ 7 ltr.
☐ 10 ltr.
bar ☐ 12 ltr.
☐ 15 ltr.
☐ Alu

☐ Luft air
☐ Nitrox _____ %

Tiefe depth	Dauer duration

Instructor **Buddies**
Signature:

No.:

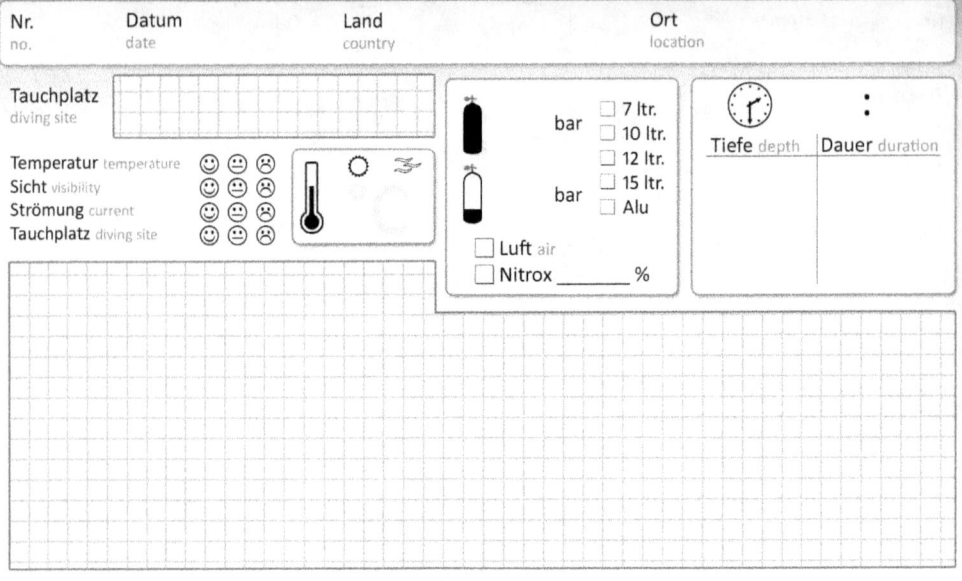

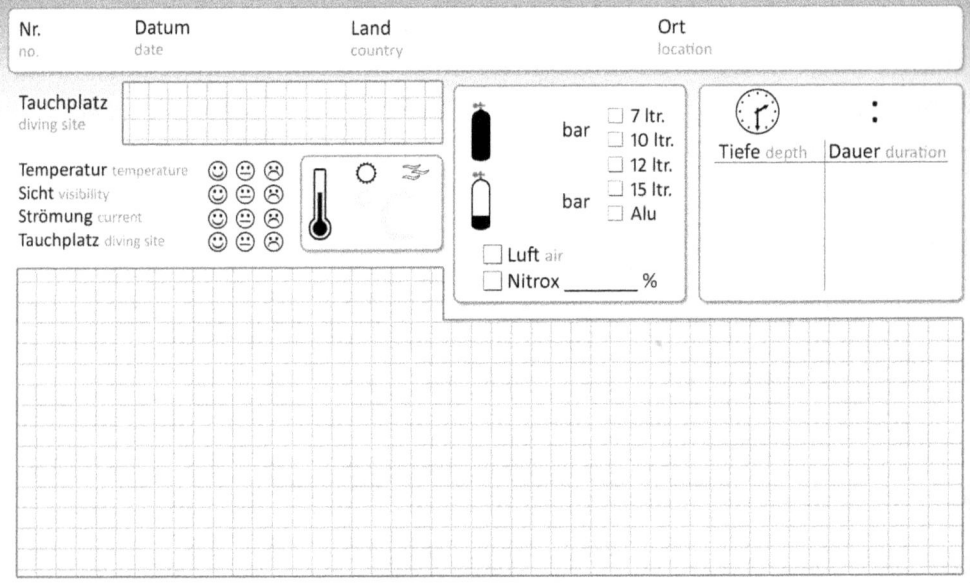

Nr. no.	Datum date	Land country		Ort location	

Tauchplatz diving site

Temperatur temperature ☺ ☺ ☹
Sicht visibility ☺ ☺ ☹
Strömung current ☺ ☺ ☹
Tauchplatz diving site ☺ ☺ ☹

bar ☐ 7 ltr.
     ☐ 10 ltr.
     ☐ 12 ltr.
bar ☐ 15 ltr.
     ☐ Alu

☐ Luft air
☐ Nitrox _____ %

Tiefe depth | Dauer duration

Instructor   **Buddies**

Signature:

No.:

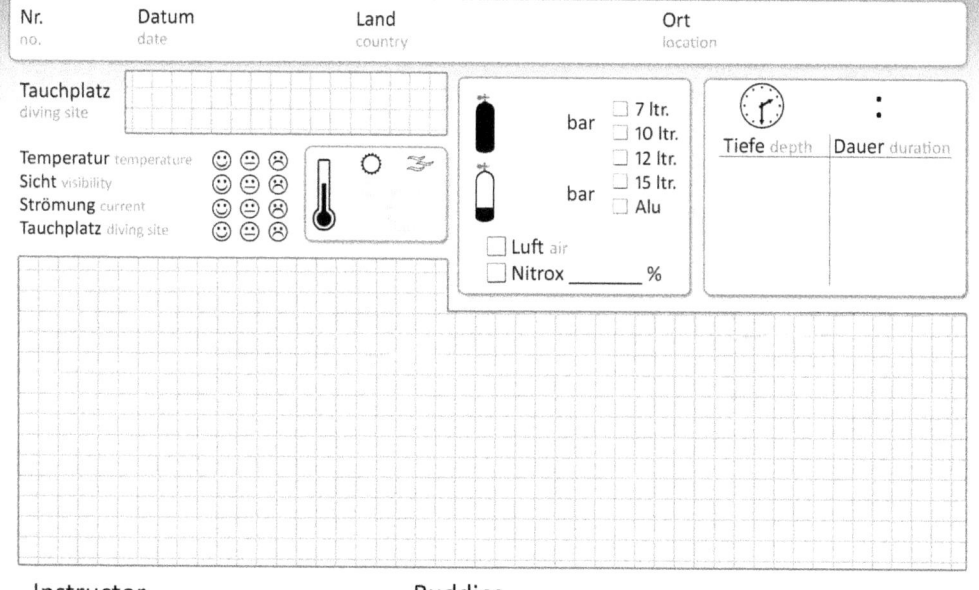

Nr. no.	Datum date	Land country		Ort location	

Tauchplatz diving site

Temperatur temperature ☺ ☺ ☹
Sicht visibility ☺ ☺ ☹
Strömung current ☺ ☺ ☹
Tauchplatz diving site ☺ ☺ ☹

bar ☐ 7 ltr.
     ☐ 10 ltr.
     ☐ 12 ltr.
bar ☐ 15 ltr.
     ☐ Alu

☐ Luft air
☐ Nitrox _____ %

Tiefe depth | Dauer duration

Instructor   **Buddies**

Signature:

No.:

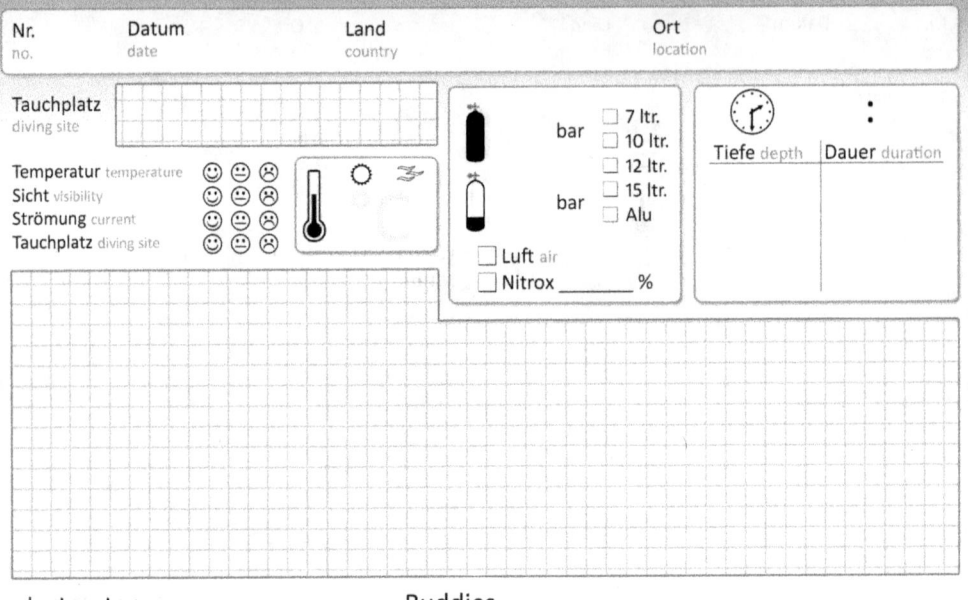

Instructor   Buddies

Signature:

No.:

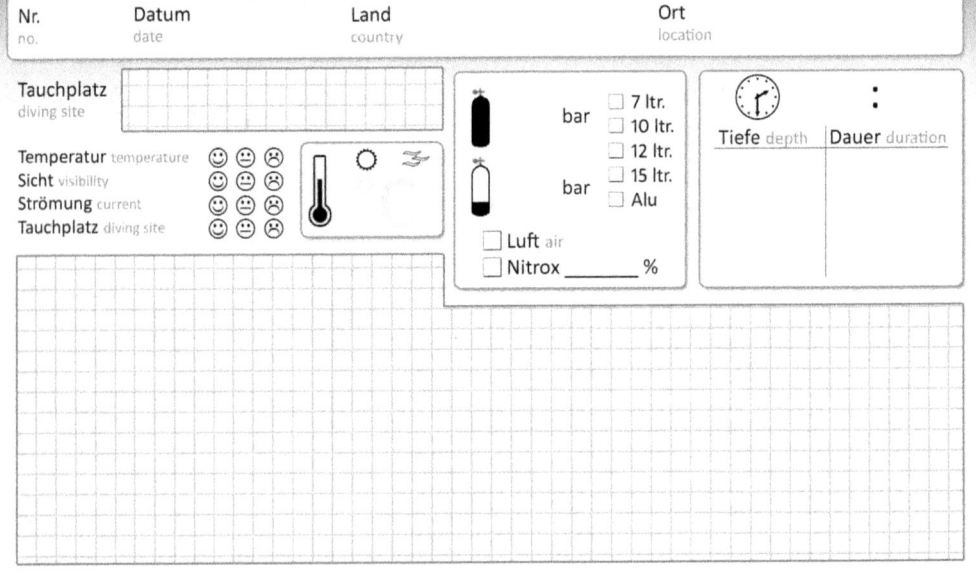

Instructor   Buddies

Signature:

No.:

Nr. no.	Datum date	Land country	Ort location

Tauchplatz diving site

Temperatur temperature ☺ 😐 ☹
Sicht visibility ☺ 😐 ☹
Strömung current ☺ 😐 ☹
Tauchplatz diving site ☺ 😐 ☹

bar ☐ 7 ltr. ☐ 10 ltr. ☐ 12 ltr.
bar ☐ 15 ltr. ☐ Alu
☐ Luft air
☐ Nitrox _____ %

Tiefe depth	Dauer duration

Instructor   Buddies
Signature:

No.:

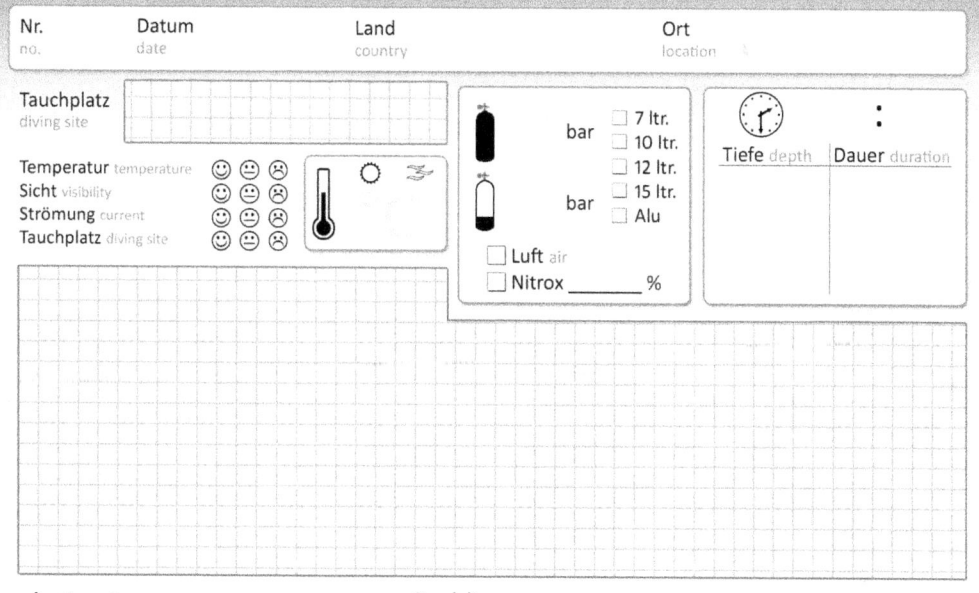

Nr. no.	Datum date	Land country	Ort location

Tauchplatz diving site

Temperatur temperature ☺ 😐 ☹
Sicht visibility ☺ 😐 ☹
Strömung current ☺ 😐 ☹
Tauchplatz diving site ☺ 😐 ☹

bar ☐ 7 ltr. ☐ 10 ltr. ☐ 12 ltr.
bar ☐ 15 ltr. ☐ Alu
☐ Luft air
☐ Nitrox _____ %

Tiefe depth	Dauer duration

Instructor   Buddies
Signature:

No.:

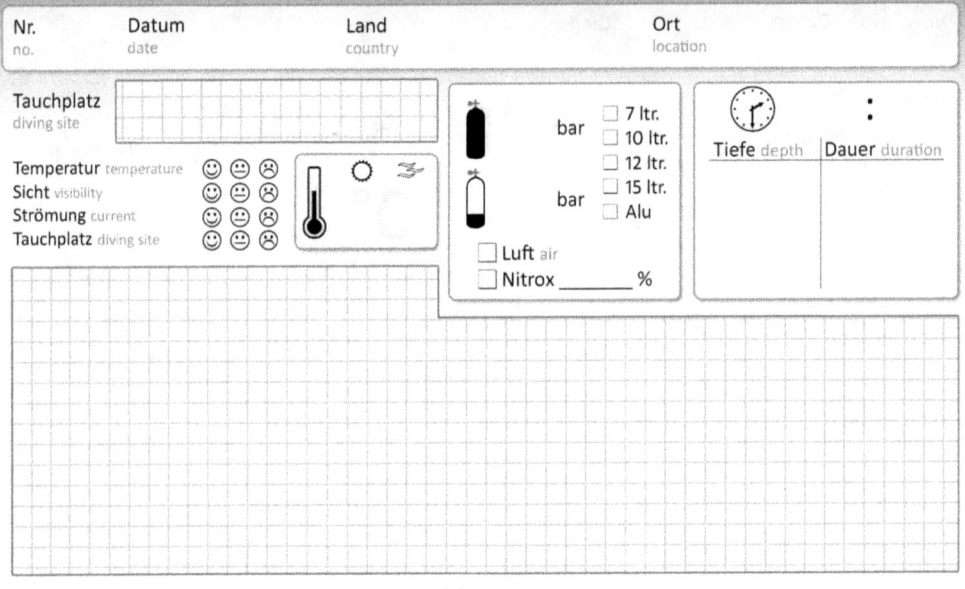

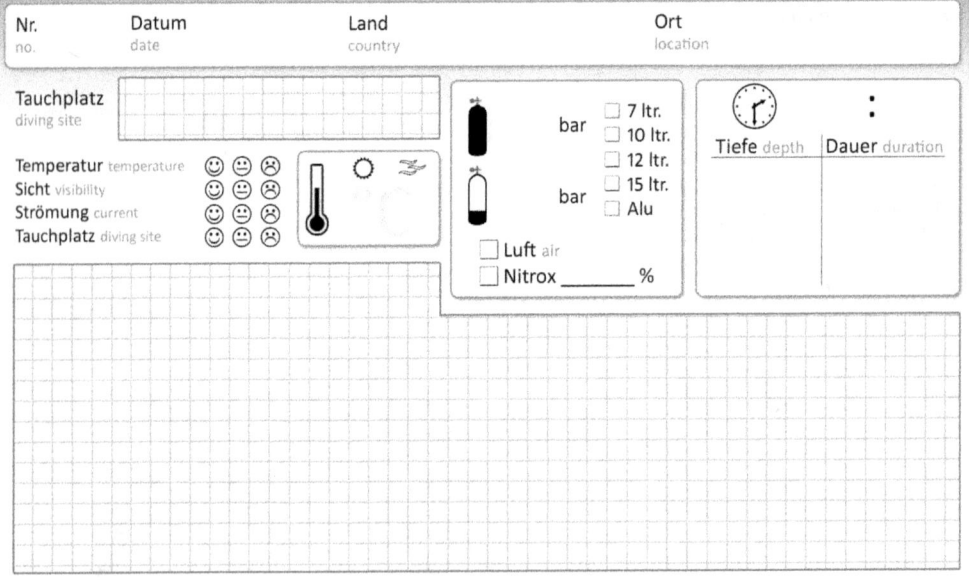

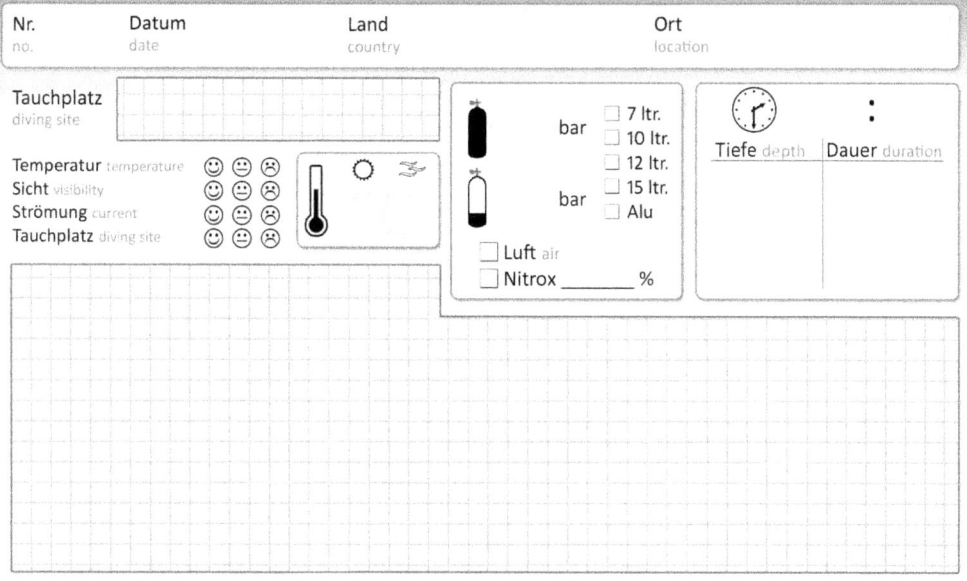

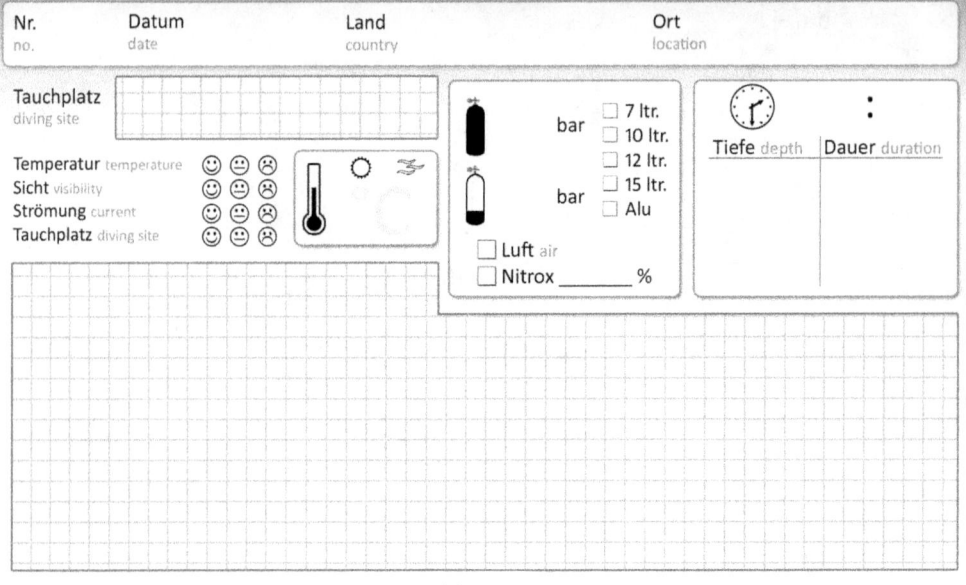

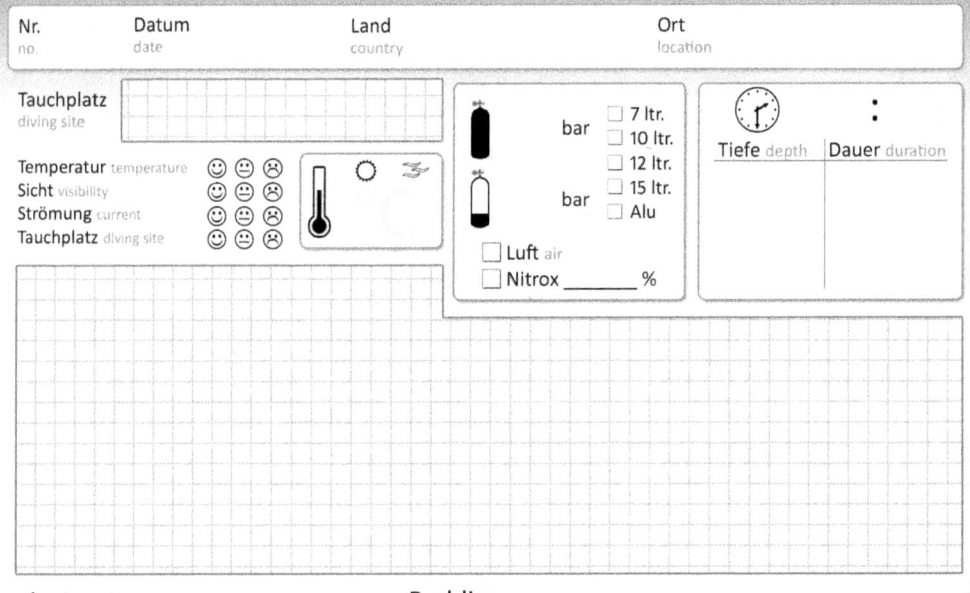

Nr. no. | Datum date | Land country | Ort location

Tauchplatz diving site

Temperatur temperature ☺ 😐 ☹
Sicht visibility ☺ 😐 ☹
Strömung current ☺ 😐 ☹
Tauchplatz diving site ☺ 😐 ☹

bar
bar

☐ 7 ltr.
☐ 10 ltr.
☐ 12 ltr.
☐ 15 ltr.
☐ Alu

☐ Luft air
☐ Nitrox ________ %

:

Tiefe depth	Dauer duration

Instructor

Signature:

No.:

Buddies

Nr. no. | Datum date | Land country | Ort location

Tauchplatz diving site

Temperatur temperature ☺ 😐 ☹
Sicht visibility ☺ 😐 ☹
Strömung current ☺ 😐 ☹
Tauchplatz diving site ☺ 😐 ☹

bar
bar

☐ 7 ltr.
☐ 10 ltr.
☐ 12 ltr.
☐ 15 ltr.
☐ Alu

☐ Luft air
☐ Nitrox ________ %

:

Tiefe depth	Dauer duration

Instructor

Signature:

No.:

Buddies

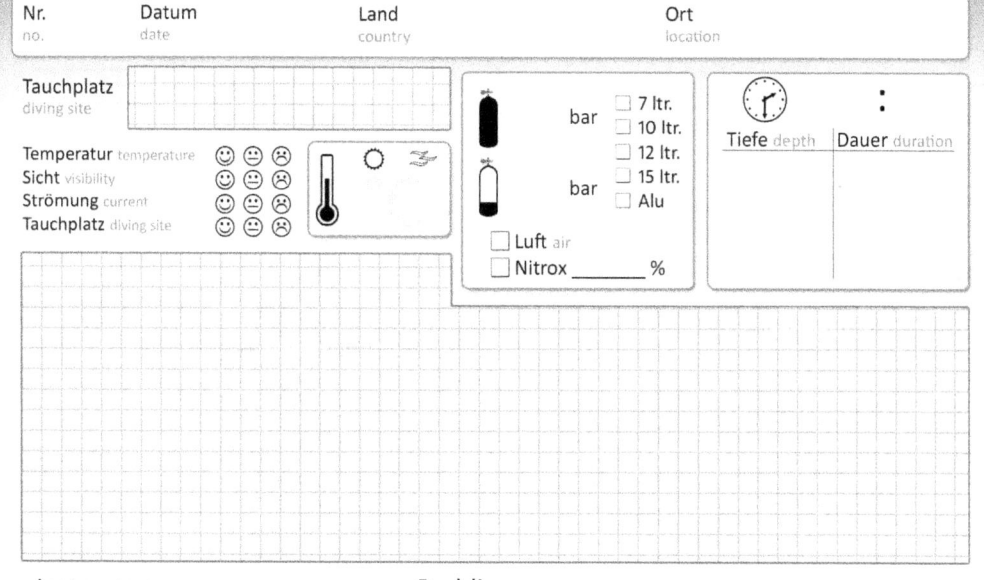

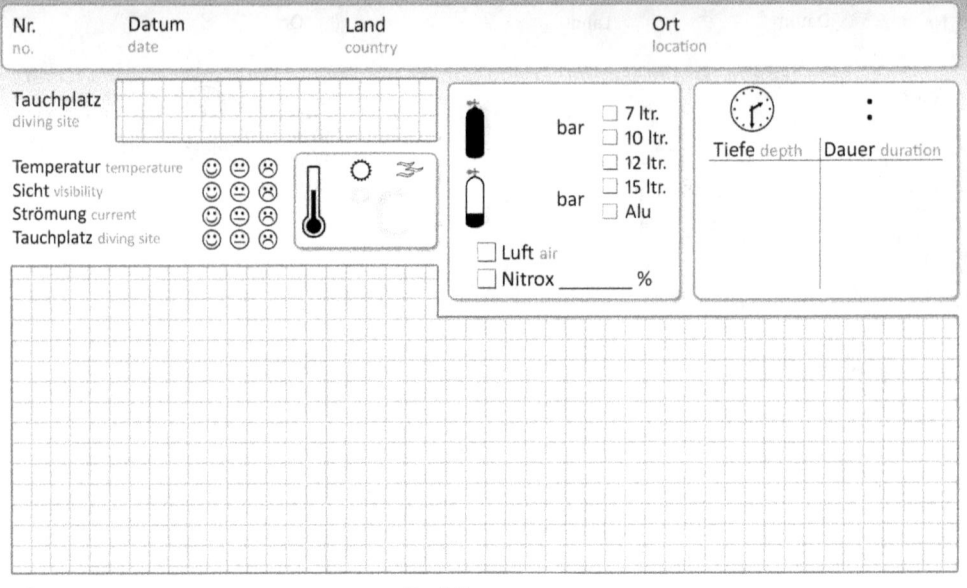

Instructor   Buddies

Signature:

No.:

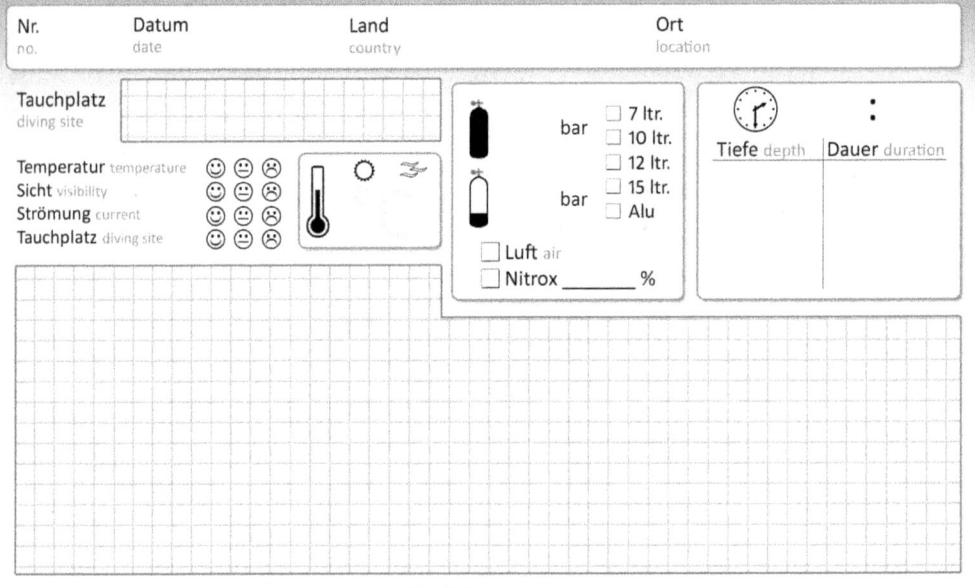

Instructor   Buddies

Signature:

No.:

Nr. no.	Datum date	Land country		Ort location	

Tauchplatz diving site

Temperatur temperature ☺ ☺ ☹
Sicht visibility ☺ ☺ ☹
Strömung current ☺ ☺ ☹
Tauchplatz diving site ☺ ☺ ☹

bar ☐ 7 ltr. ☐ 10 ltr. ☐ 12 ltr.
bar ☐ 15 ltr. ☐ Alu
☐ Luft air
☐ Nitrox _____ %

Tiefe depth	Dauer duration

Instructor   Buddies

Signature:

No.:

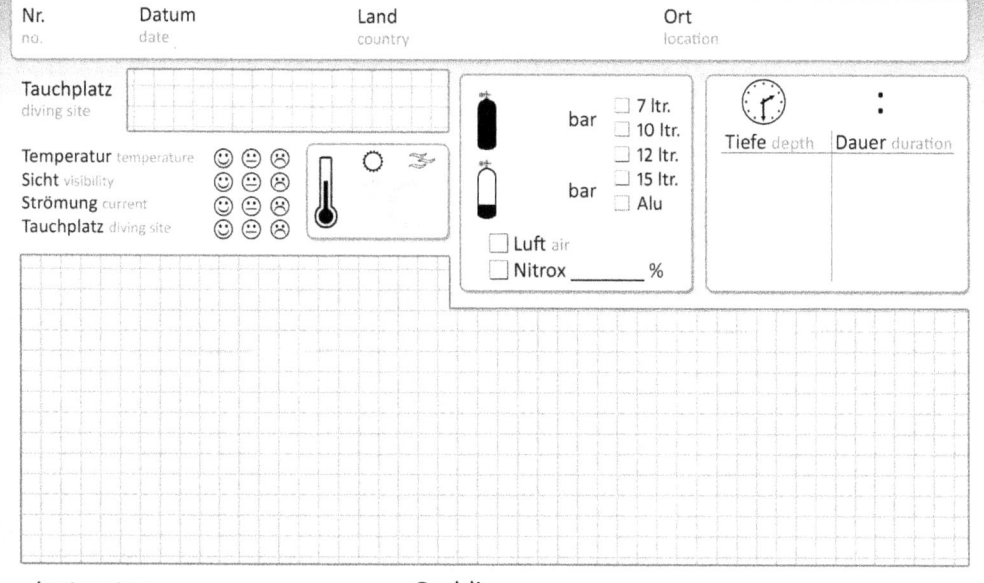

Nr. no.	Datum date	Land country		Ort location	

Tauchplatz diving site

Temperatur temperature ☺ ☺ ☹
Sicht visibility ☺ ☺ ☹
Strömung current ☺ ☺ ☹
Tauchplatz diving site ☺ ☺ ☹

bar ☐ 7 ltr. ☐ 10 ltr. ☐ 12 ltr.
bar ☐ 15 ltr. ☐ Alu
☐ Luft air
☐ Nitrox _____ %

Tiefe depth	Dauer duration

Instructor   Buddies

Signature:

No.:

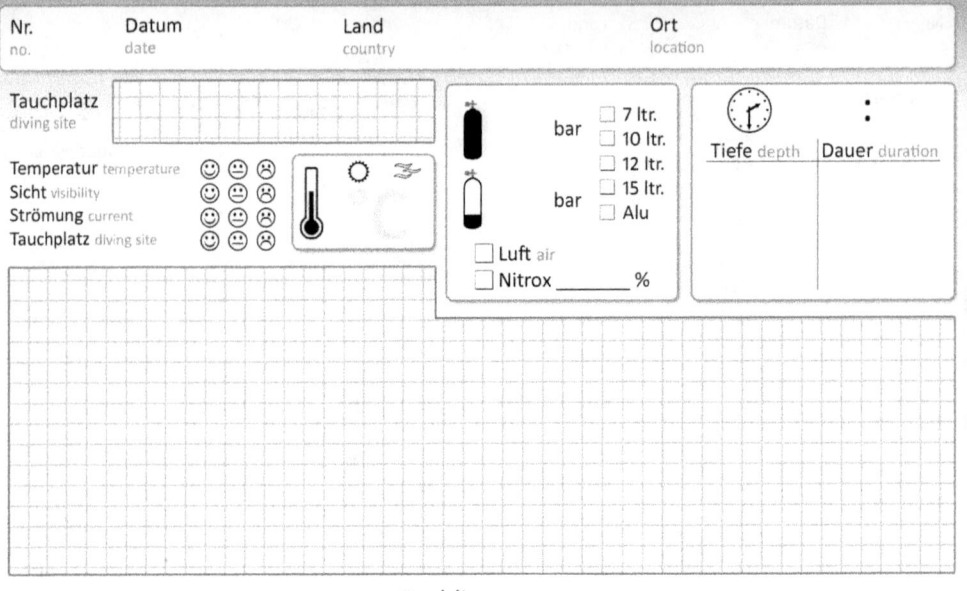

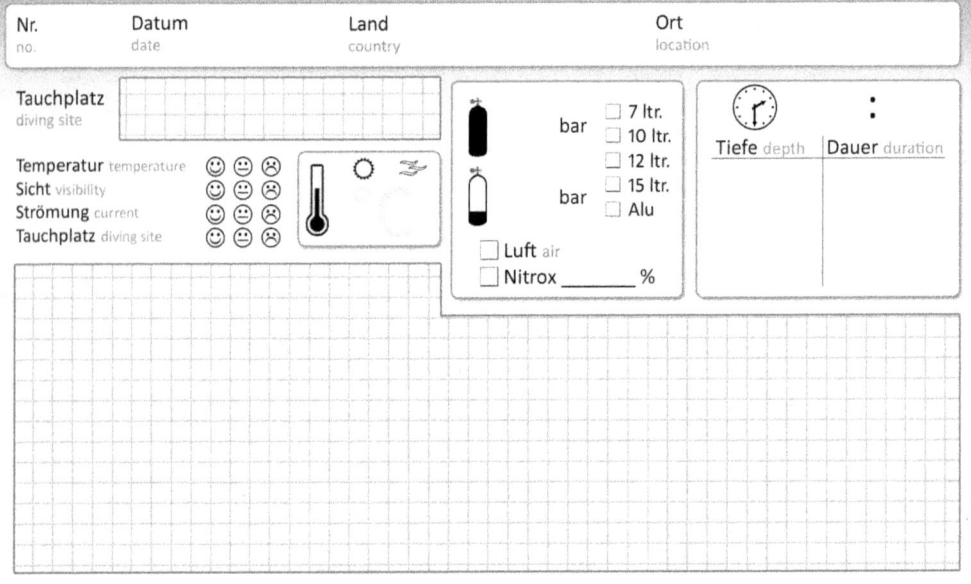

| Nr. no. | Datum date | Land country | Ort location |

Tauchplatz diving site

Temperatur temperature
Sicht visibility
Strömung current
Tauchplatz diving site

bar
bar
- [ ] 7 ltr.
- [ ] 10 ltr.
- [ ] 12 ltr.
- [ ] 15 ltr.
- [ ] Alu
- [ ] Luft air
- [ ] Nitrox _____ %

Tiefe depth | Dauer duration

Instructor   **Buddies**
Signature:

No.:

| Nr. no. | Datum date | Land country | Ort location |

Tauchplatz diving site

Temperatur temperature
Sicht visibility
Strömung current
Tauchplatz diving site

bar
bar
- [ ] 7 ltr.
- [ ] 10 ltr.
- [ ] 12 ltr.
- [ ] 15 ltr.
- [ ] Alu
- [ ] Luft air
- [ ] Nitrox _____ %

Tiefe depth | Dauer duration

Instructor   **Buddies**
Signature:

No.:

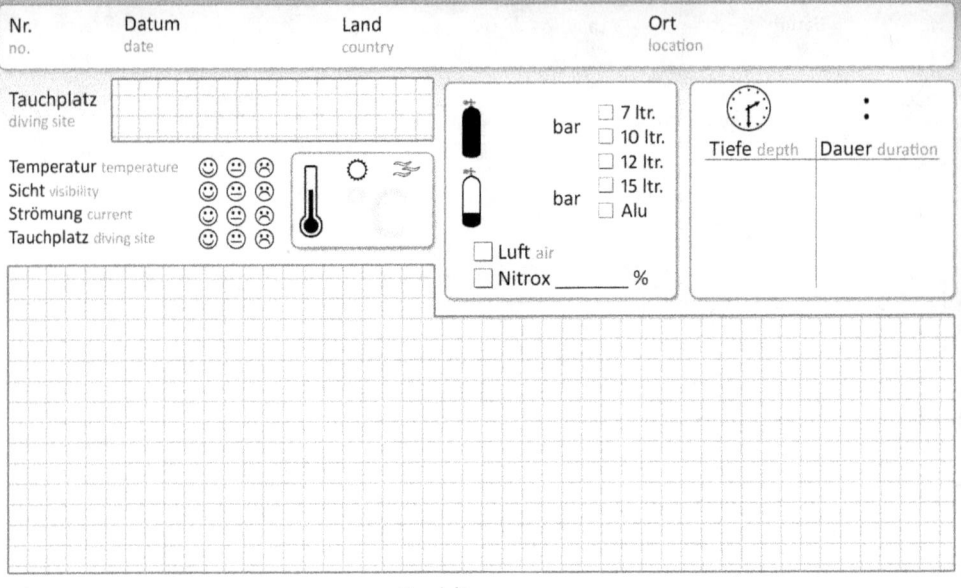

Instructor   Buddies
Signature:

No.:

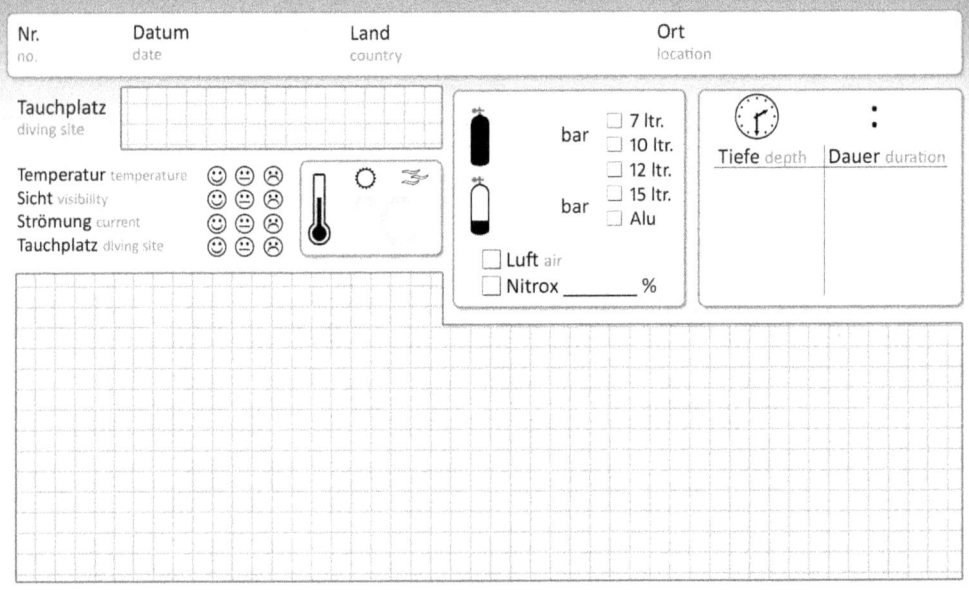

Instructor   Buddies
Signature:

No.:

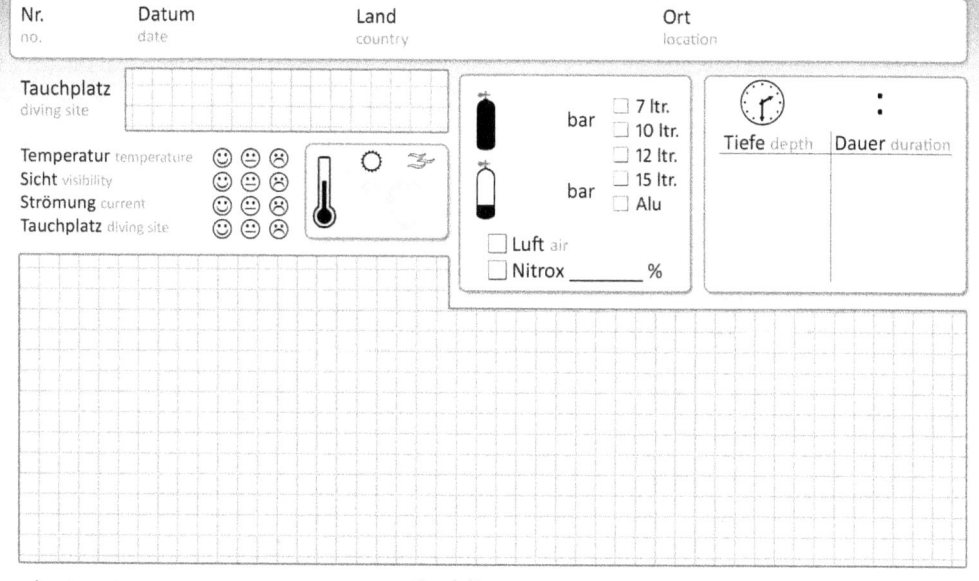

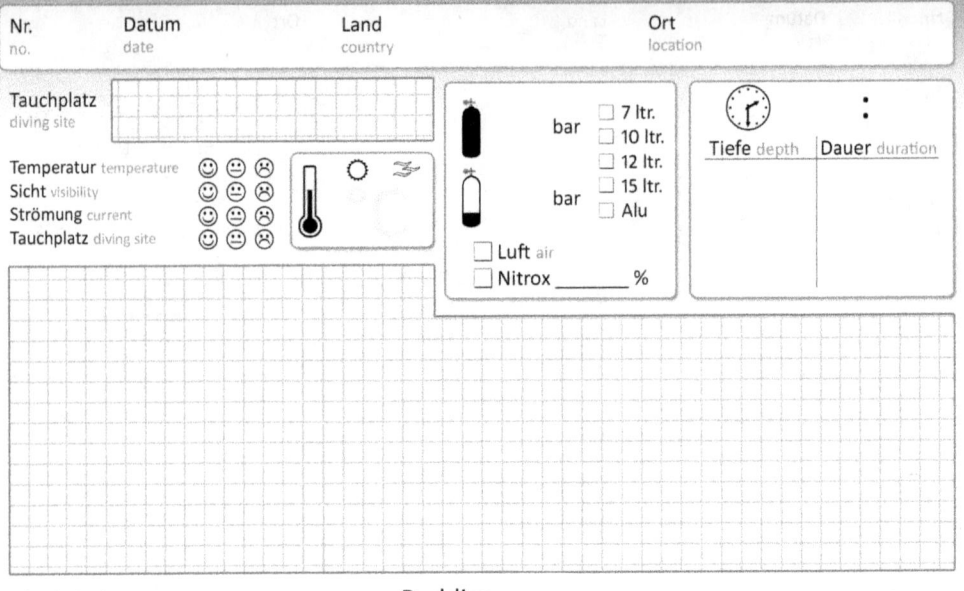

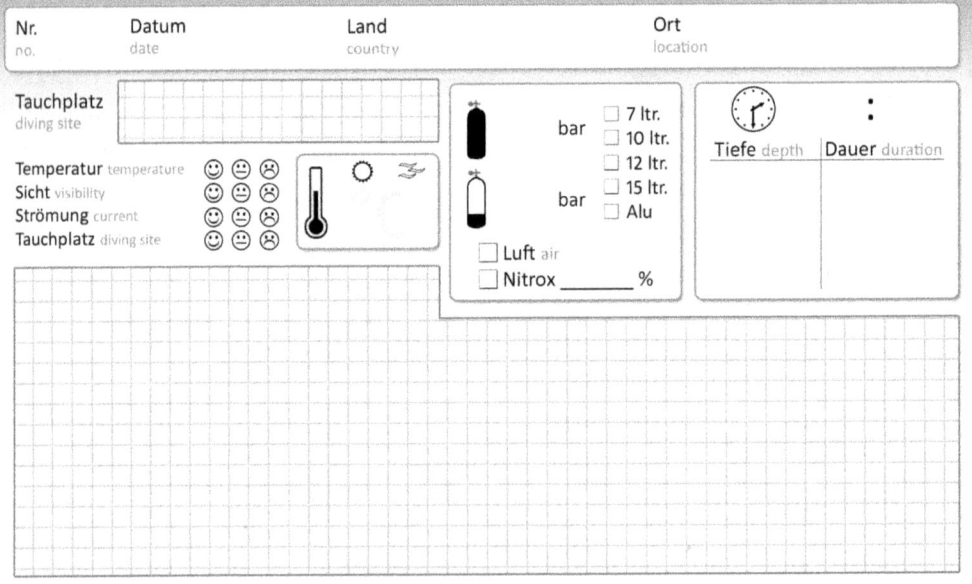

Nr. no.	Datum date	Land country	Ort location

Tauchplatz diving site

Temperatur temperature ☺ 😐 ☹
Sicht visibility ☺ 😐 ☹
Strömung current ☺ 😐 ☹
Tauchplatz diving site ☺ 😐 ☹

bar ☐ 7 ltr. ☐ 10 ltr. ☐ 12 ltr.
bar ☐ 15 ltr. ☐ Alu
☐ Luft air
☐ Nitrox _____ %

Tiefe depth | Dauer duration

Instructor
Signature:

Buddies

No.:

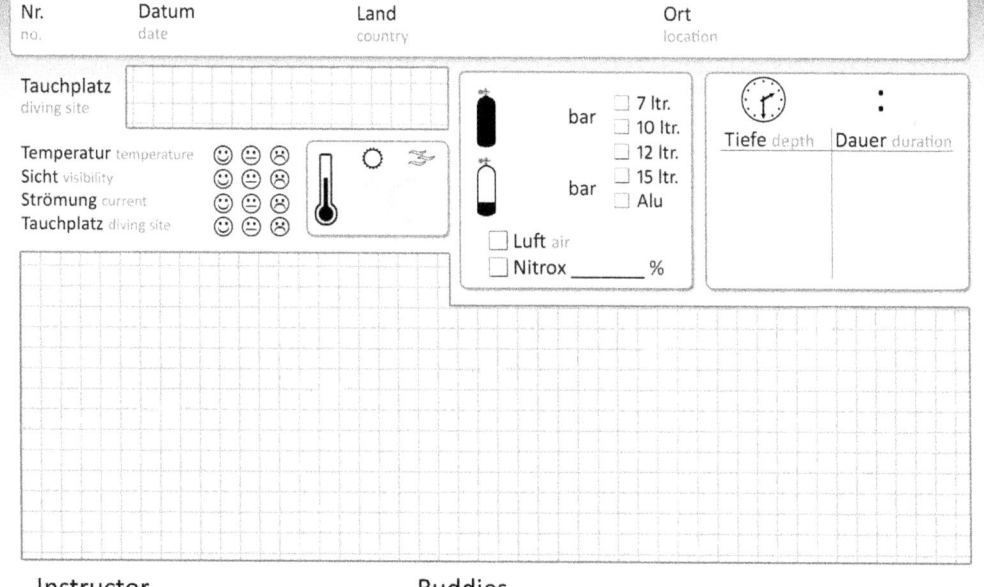

Nr. no.	Datum date	Land country	Ort location

Tauchplatz diving site

Temperatur temperature ☺ 😐 ☹
Sicht visibility ☺ 😐 ☹
Strömung current ☺ 😐 ☹
Tauchplatz diving site ☺ 😐 ☹

bar ☐ 7 ltr. ☐ 10 ltr. ☐ 12 ltr.
bar ☐ 15 ltr. ☐ Alu
☐ Luft air
☐ Nitrox _____ %

Tiefe depth | Dauer duration

Instructor
Signature:

Buddies

No.:

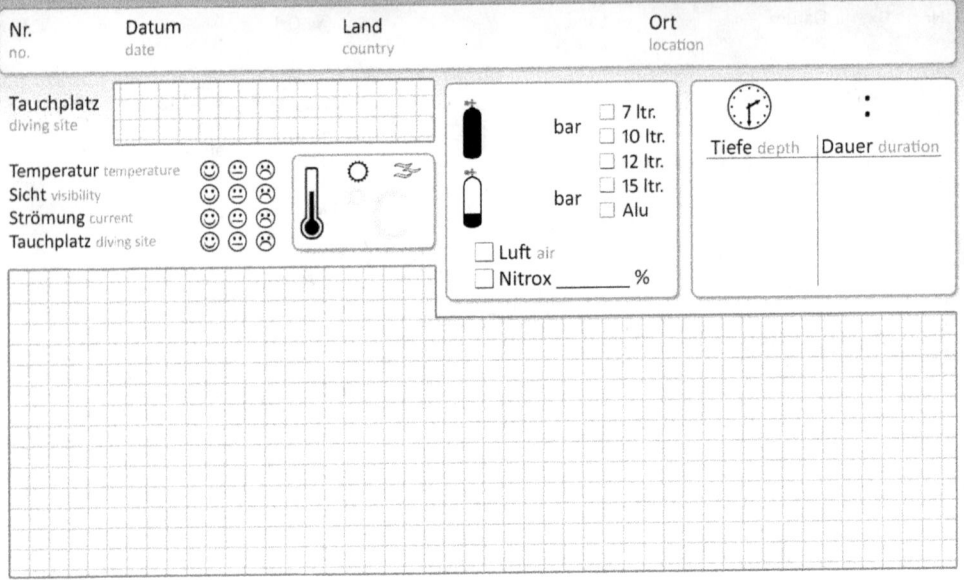

Instructor

Buddies

Signature:

No.:

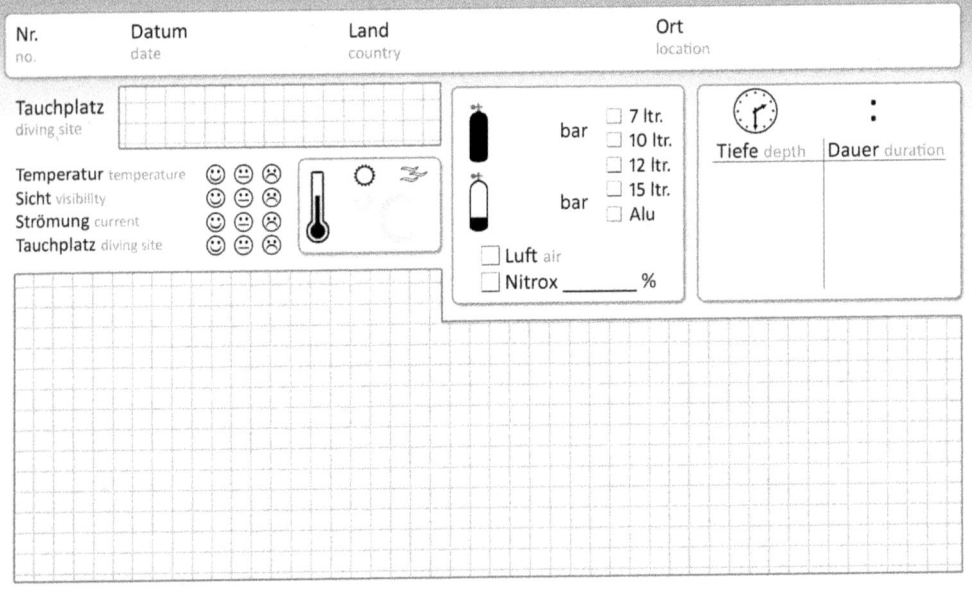

Instructor

Buddies

Signature:

No.:

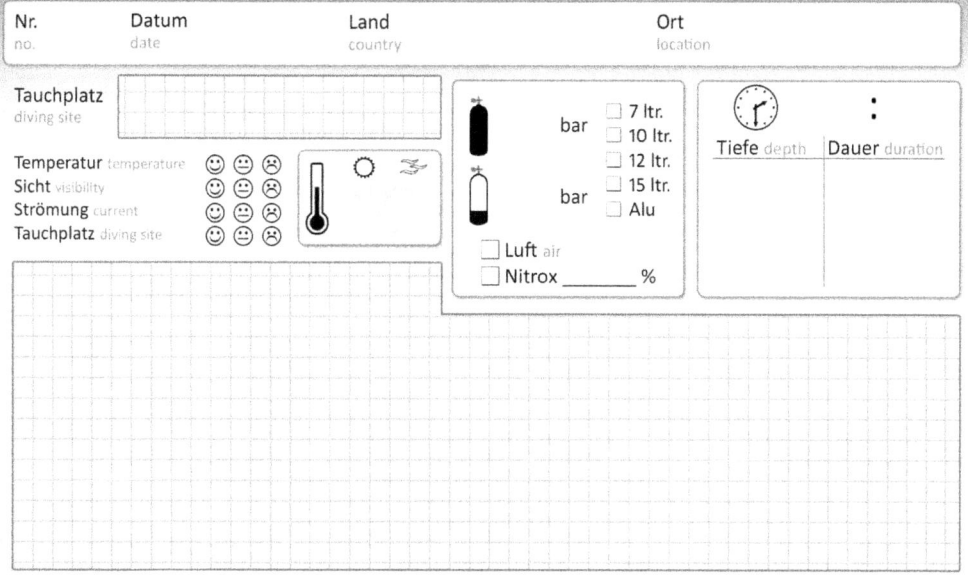

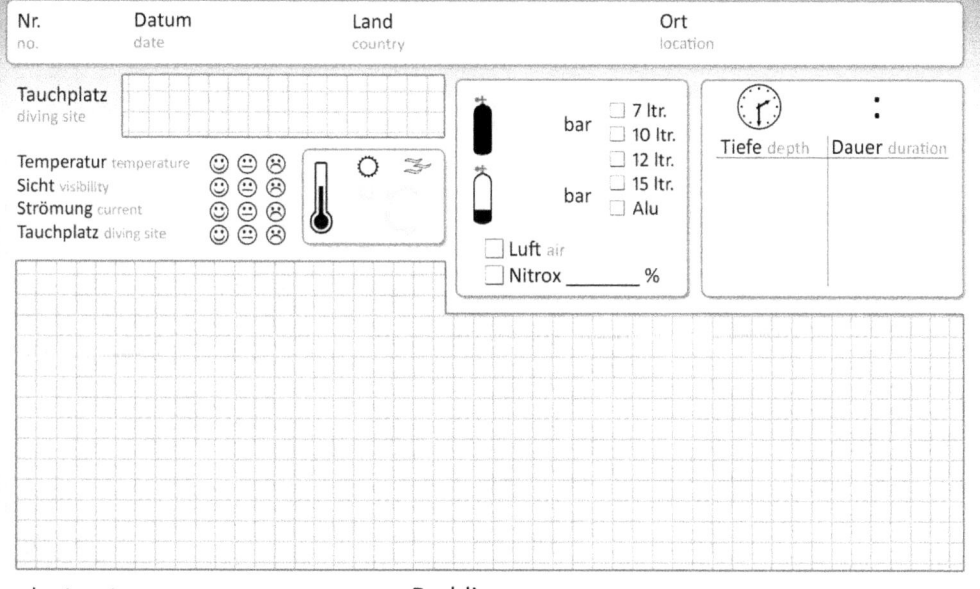

Nr. no.	Datum date	Land country		Ort location	

Tauchplatz diving site

Temperatur temperature ☺ 😐 ☹
Sicht visibility ☺ 😐 ☹
Strömung current ☺ 😐 ☹
Tauchplatz diving site ☺ 😐 ☹

bar ☐ 7 ltr. ☐ 10 ltr. ☐ 12 ltr.
bar ☐ 15 ltr. ☐ Alu
☐ Luft air
☐ Nitrox _____ %

Tiefe depth | **Dauer** duration

Instructor   Buddies
Signature:

No.:

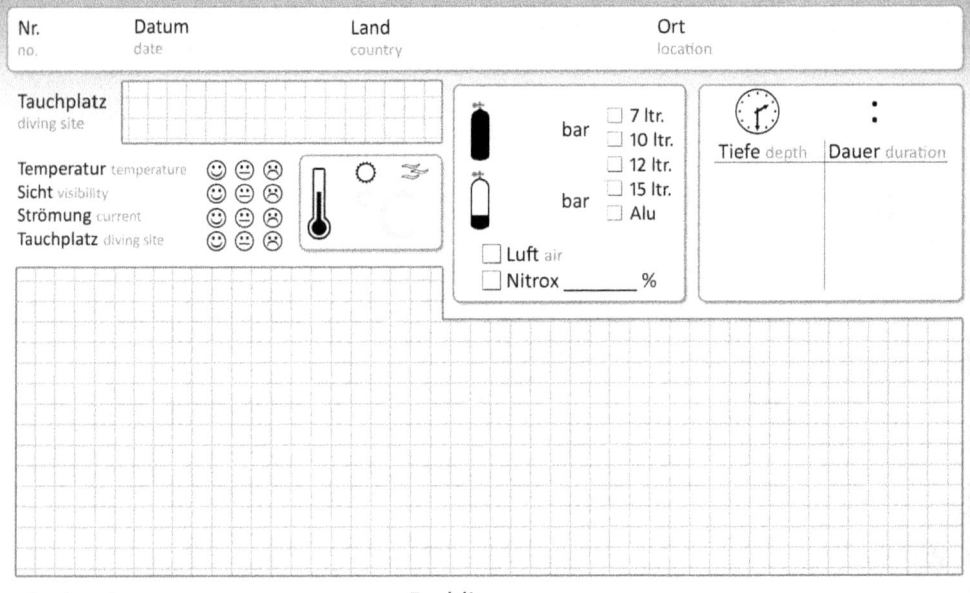

Nr. no.	Datum date	Land country		Ort location	

Tauchplatz diving site

Temperatur temperature ☺ 😐 ☹
Sicht visibility ☺ 😐 ☹
Strömung current ☺ 😐 ☹
Tauchplatz diving site ☺ 😐 ☹

bar ☐ 7 ltr. ☐ 10 ltr. ☐ 12 ltr.
bar ☐ 15 ltr. ☐ Alu
☐ Luft air
☐ Nitrox _____ %

Tiefe depth | **Dauer** duration

Instructor   Buddies
Signature:

No.:

Nr. no. | Datum date | Land country | Ort location

Tauchplatz diving site

Temperatur temperature
Sicht visibility
Strömung current
Tauchplatz diving site

bar
bar

☐ 7 ltr.
☐ 10 ltr.
☐ 12 ltr.
☐ 15 ltr.
☐ Alu

☐ Luft air
☐ Nitrox _______ %

:

Tiefe depth	Dauer duration

Instructor

Signature:

No.:

Buddies

Nr. no. | Datum date | Land country | Ort location

Tauchplatz diving site

Temperatur temperature
Sicht visibility
Strömung current
Tauchplatz diving site

bar
bar

☐ 7 ltr.
☐ 10 ltr.
☐ 12 ltr.
☐ 15 ltr.
☐ Alu

☐ Luft air
☐ Nitrox _______ %

:

Tiefe depth	Dauer duration

Instructor

Signature:

No.:

Buddies

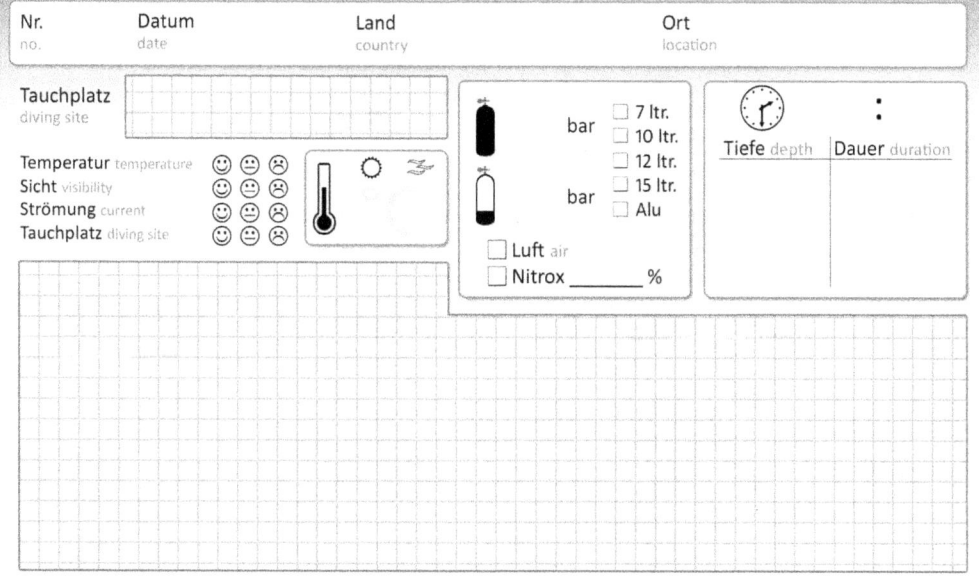

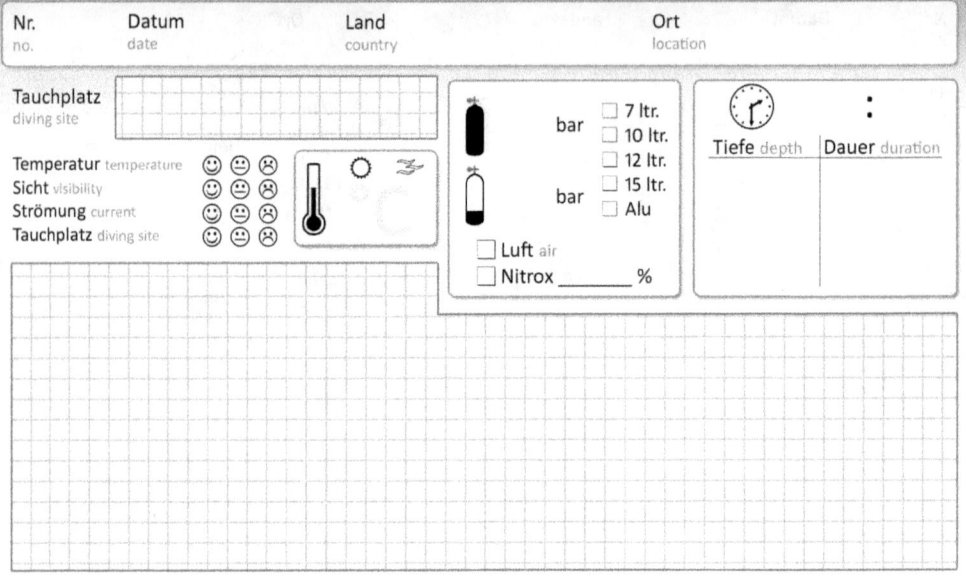

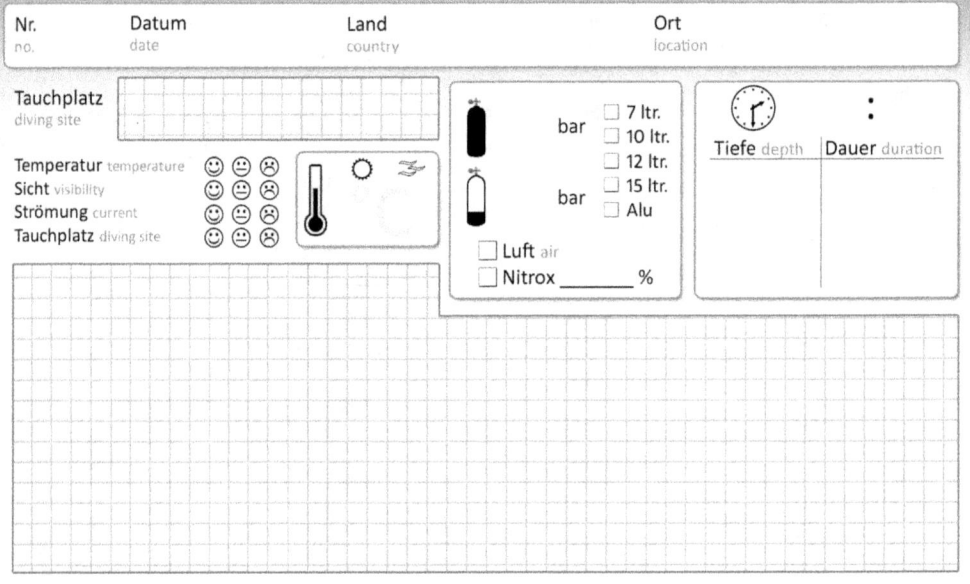

Nr. no.	Datum date	Land country	Ort location

Tauchplatz diving site

Temperatur temperature ☺ ☻ ☹
Sicht visibility ☺ ☻ ☹
Strömung current ☺ ☻ ☹
Tauchplatz diving site ☺ ☻ ☹

bar ☐ 7 ltr.
☐ 10 ltr.
☐ 12 ltr.
bar ☐ 15 ltr.
☐ Alu
☐ Luft air
☐ Nitrox _____ %

Tiefe depth | Dauer duration

Instructor   Buddies
Signature:

No.:

Nr. no.	Datum date	Land country	Ort location

Tauchplatz diving site

Temperatur temperature ☺ ☻ ☹
Sicht visibility ☺ ☻ ☹
Strömung current ☺ ☻ ☹
Tauchplatz diving site ☺ ☻ ☹

bar ☐ 7 ltr.
☐ 10 ltr.
☐ 12 ltr.
bar ☐ 15 ltr.
☐ Alu
☐ Luft air
☐ Nitrox _____ %

Tiefe depth | Dauer duration

Instructor   Buddies
Signature:

No.:

Nr. no.	Datum date	Land country		Ort location	

Tauchplatz diving site

Temperatur temperature ☺ ☻ ☹
Sicht visibility ☺ ☻ ☹
Strömung current ☺ ☻ ☹
Tauchplatz diving site ☺ ☻ ☹

bar ☐ 7 ltr. ☐ 10 ltr. ☐ 12 ltr.
bar ☐ 15 ltr. ☐ Alu
☐ Luft air
☐ Nitrox _____ %

Tiefe depth	Dauer duration

Instructor   Buddies

Signature:

No.:

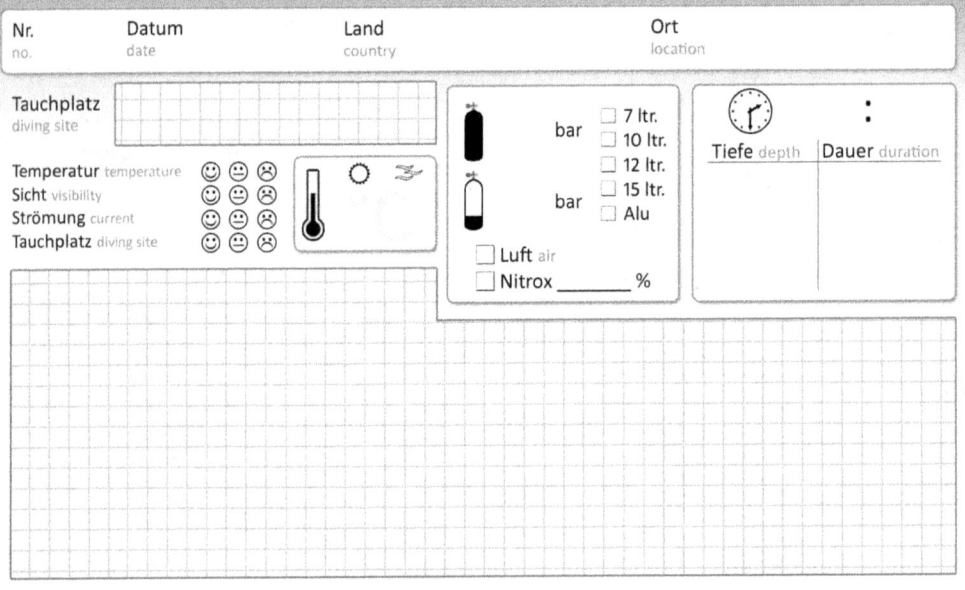

Nr. no.	Datum date	Land country		Ort location	

Tauchplatz diving site

Temperatur temperature ☺ ☻ ☹
Sicht visibility ☺ ☻ ☹
Strömung current ☺ ☻ ☹
Tauchplatz diving site ☺ ☻ ☹

bar ☐ 7 ltr. ☐ 10 ltr. ☐ 12 ltr.
bar ☐ 15 ltr. ☐ Alu
☐ Luft air
☐ Nitrox _____ %

Tiefe depth	Dauer duration

Instructor   Buddies

Signature:

No.:

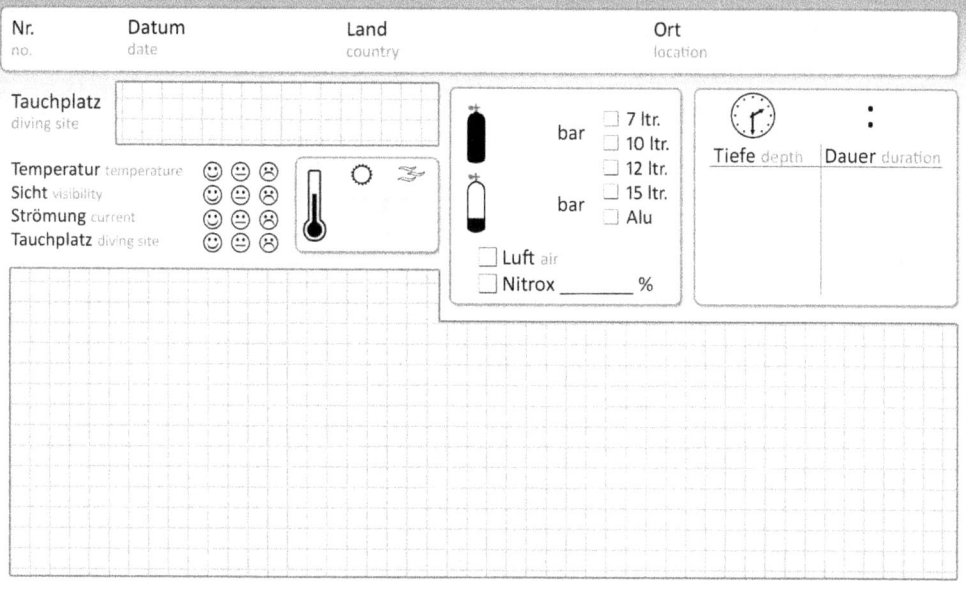

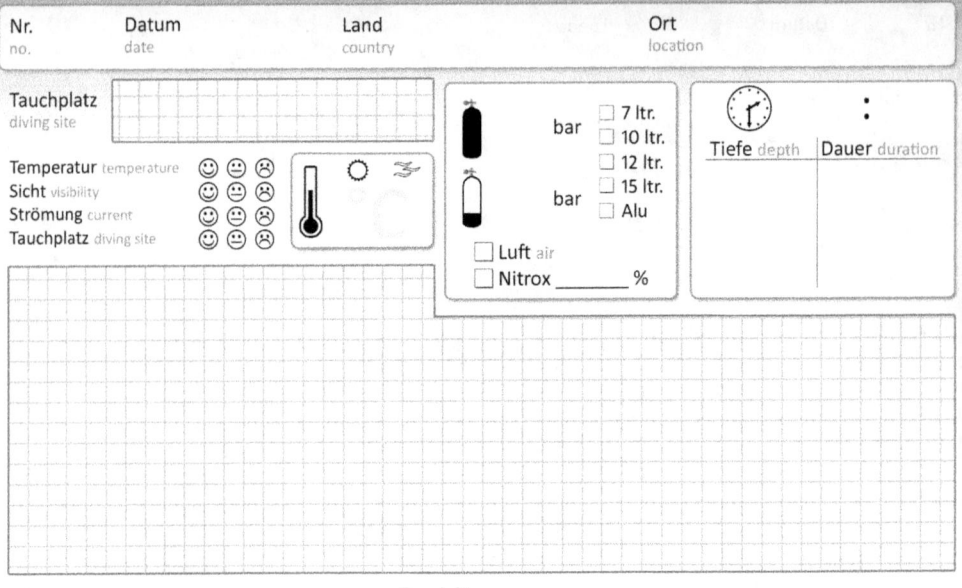

Instructor   Buddies

Signature:

No.:

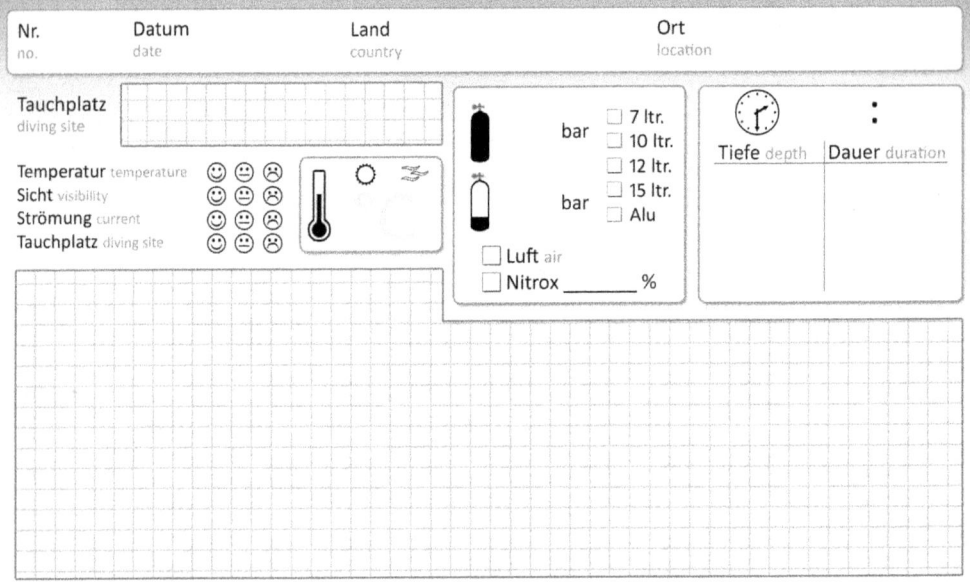

Instructor   Buddies

Signature:

No.:

Nr. no.	Datum date	Land country	Ort location

Tauchplatz diving site

Temperatur temperature ☺ 😐 ☹
Sicht visibility ☺ 😐 ☹
Strömung current ☺ 😐 ☹
Tauchplatz diving site ☺ 😐 ☹

bar ☐ 7 ltr.
☐ 10 ltr.
☐ 12 ltr.
bar ☐ 15 ltr.
☐ Alu

☐ Luft air
☐ Nitrox _____ %

Tiefe depth | **Dauer** duration

Instructor   Buddies
Signature:

No.:

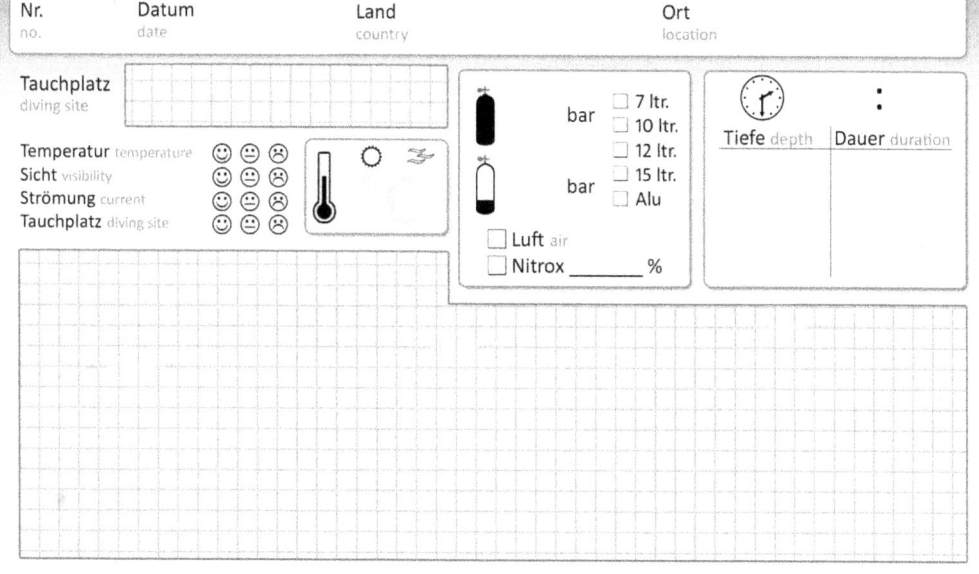

Nr. no.	Datum date	Land country	Ort location

Tauchplatz diving site

Temperatur temperature ☺ 😐 ☹
Sicht visibility ☺ 😐 ☹
Strömung current ☺ 😐 ☹
Tauchplatz diving site ☺ 😐 ☹

bar ☐ 7 ltr.
☐ 10 ltr.
☐ 12 ltr.
bar ☐ 15 ltr.
☐ Alu

☐ Luft air
☐ Nitrox _____ %

Tiefe depth | **Dauer** duration

Instructor   Buddies
Signature:

No.:

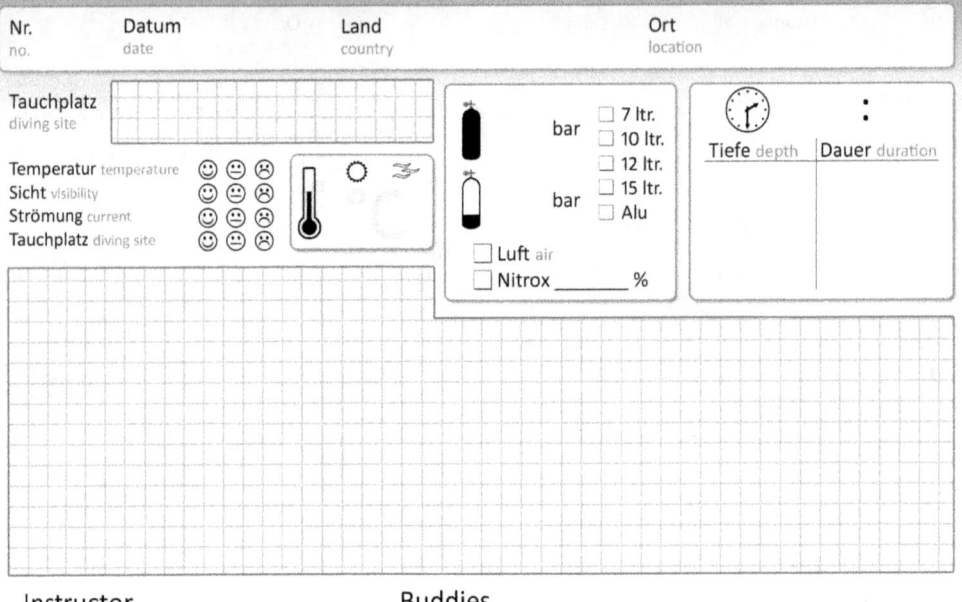

Instructor Buddies
Signature:

No.:

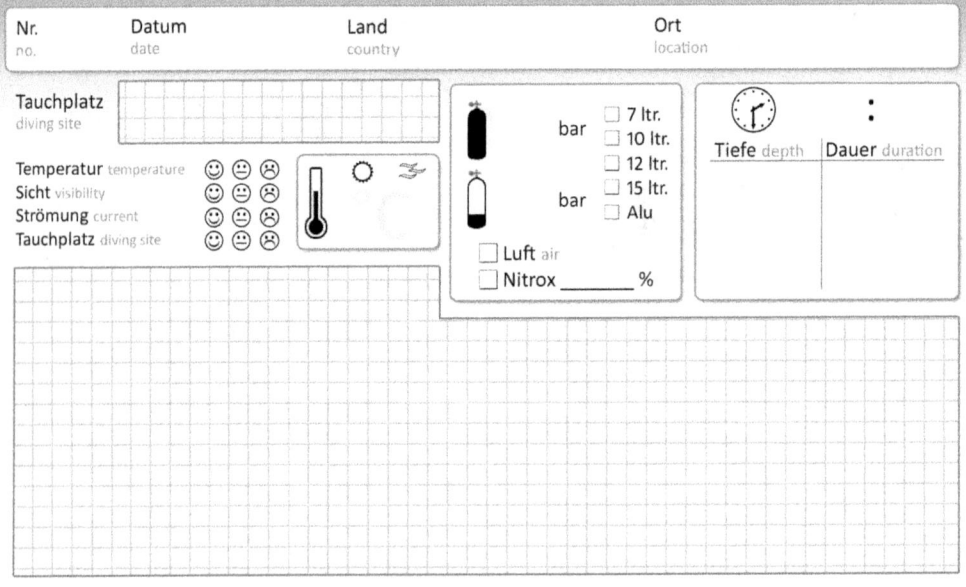

Instructor Buddies
Signature:

No.:

Nr. no.	Datum date	Land country		Ort location	

Tauchplatz diving site

Temperatur temperature ☺ 😐 ☹
Sicht visibility ☺ 😐 ☹
Strömung current ☺ 😐 ☹
Tauchplatz diving site ☺ 😐 ☹

bar ☐ 7 ltr. ☐ 10 ltr. ☐ 12 ltr.
bar ☐ 15 ltr. ☐ Alu
☐ Luft air
☐ Nitrox _____ %

Tiefe depth | Dauer duration

Instructor
Signature:

Buddies

No.:

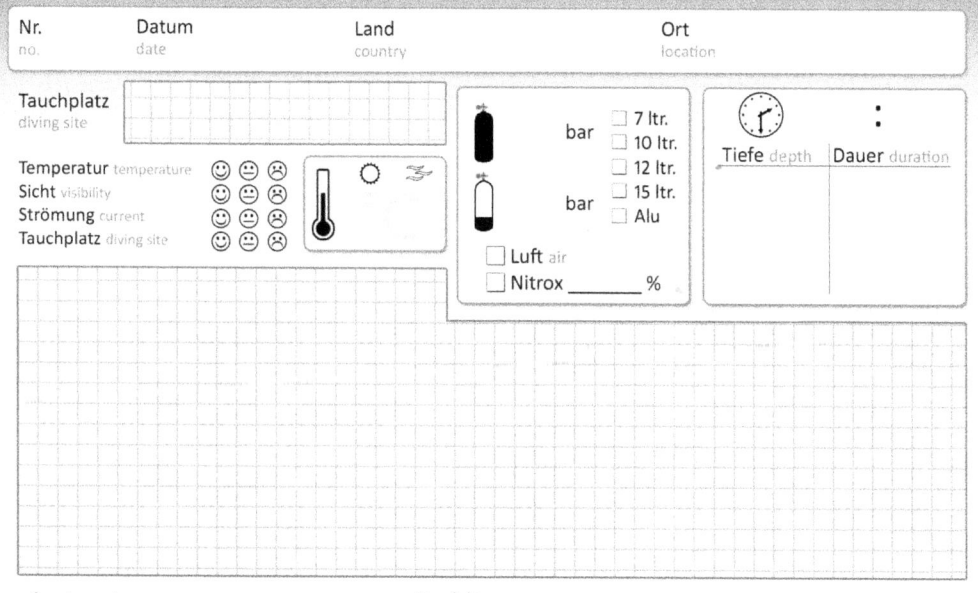

Nr. no.	Datum date	Land country		Ort location	

Tauchplatz diving site

Temperatur temperature ☺ 😐 ☹
Sicht visibility ☺ 😐 ☹
Strömung current ☺ 😐 ☹
Tauchplatz diving site ☺ 😐 ☹

bar ☐ 7 ltr. ☐ 10 ltr. ☐ 12 ltr.
bar ☐ 15 ltr. ☐ Alu
☐ Luft air
☐ Nitrox _____ %

Tiefe depth | Dauer duration

Instructor
Signature:

Buddies

No.:

Nr. no. | Datum date | Land country | Ort location

Tauchplatz diving site

Temperatur temperature ☺ 😐 ☹
Sicht visibility ☺ 😐 ☹
Strömung current ☺ 😐 ☹
Tauchplatz diving site ☺ 😐 ☹

bar ☐ 7 ltr.
☐ 10 ltr.
☐ 12 ltr.
bar ☐ 15 ltr.
☐ Alu

☐ Luft air
☐ Nitrox ________ %

:

Tiefe depth	Dauer duration

Instructor

Signature:

No.:

Buddies

Nr. no. | Datum date | Land country | Ort location

Tauchplatz diving site

Temperatur temperature ☺ 😐 ☹
Sicht visibility ☺ 😐 ☹
Strömung current ☺ 😐 ☹
Tauchplatz diving site ☺ 😐 ☹

bar ☐ 7 ltr.
☐ 10 ltr.
☐ 12 ltr.
bar ☐ 15 ltr.
☐ Alu

☐ Luft air
☐ Nitrox ________ %

:

Tiefe depth	Dauer duration

Instructor

Signature:

No.:

Buddies

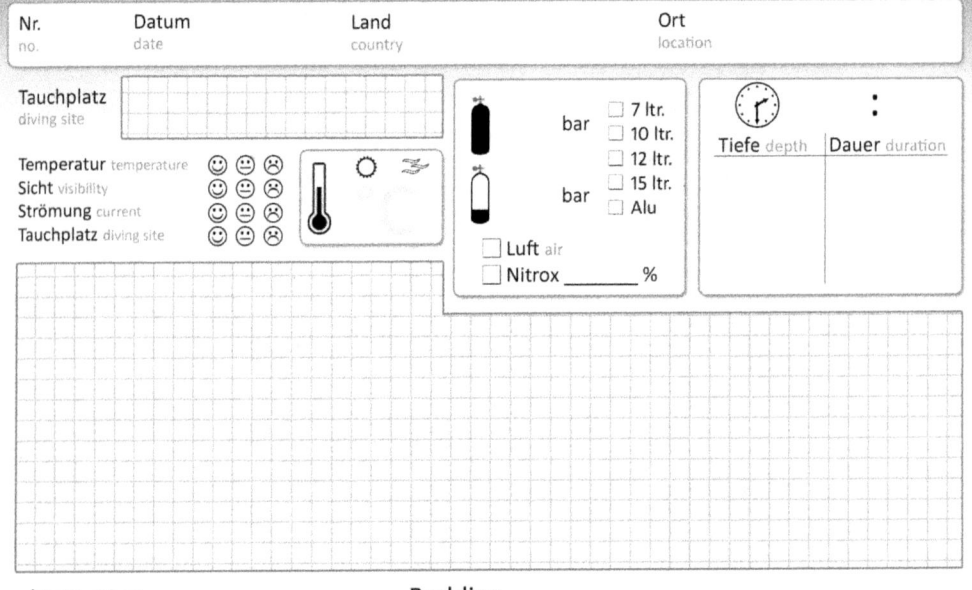

Nr. no.	Datum date	Land country		Ort location

Tauchplatz diving site

Temperatur temperature
Sicht visibility
Strömung current
Tauchplatz diving site

bar
bar

☐ 7 ltr.
☐ 10 ltr.
☐ 12 ltr.
☐ 15 ltr.
☐ Alu

☐ Luft air
☐ Nitrox _____ %

Tiefe depth | **Dauer** duration

Instructor   Buddies
Signature:

No.:

Nr. no.	Datum date	Land country		Ort location

Tauchplatz diving site

Temperatur temperature
Sicht visibility
Strömung current
Tauchplatz diving site

bar
bar

☐ 7 ltr.
☐ 10 ltr.
☐ 12 ltr.
☐ 15 ltr.
☐ Alu

☐ Luft air
☐ Nitrox _____ %

Tiefe depth | **Dauer** duration

Instructor   Buddies
Signature:

No.:

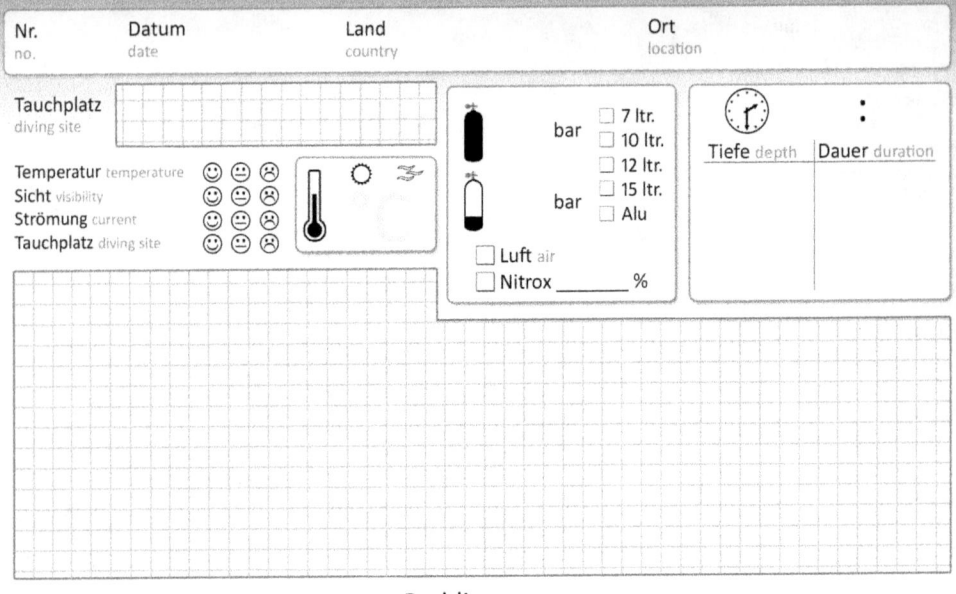

Instructor   Buddies

Signature:

No.:

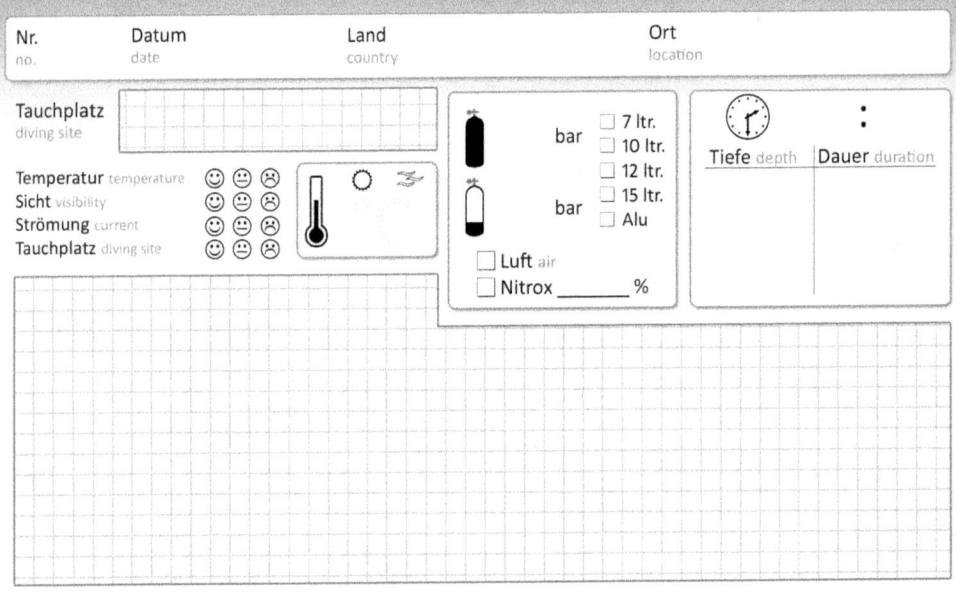

Instructor   Buddies

Signature:

No.:

Nr. no.	Datum date	Land country		Ort location		

Tauchplatz diving site

Temperatur temperature ☺ ☻ ☹
Sicht visibility ☺ ☻ ☹
Strömung current ☺ ☻ ☹
Tauchplatz diving site ☺ ☻ ☹

bar
bar

☐ 7 ltr.
☐ 10 ltr.
☐ 12 ltr.
☐ 15 ltr.
☐ Alu

☐ Luft air
☐ Nitrox _____ %

Tiefe depth | Dauer duration

Instructor   **Buddies**
Signature:

No.:

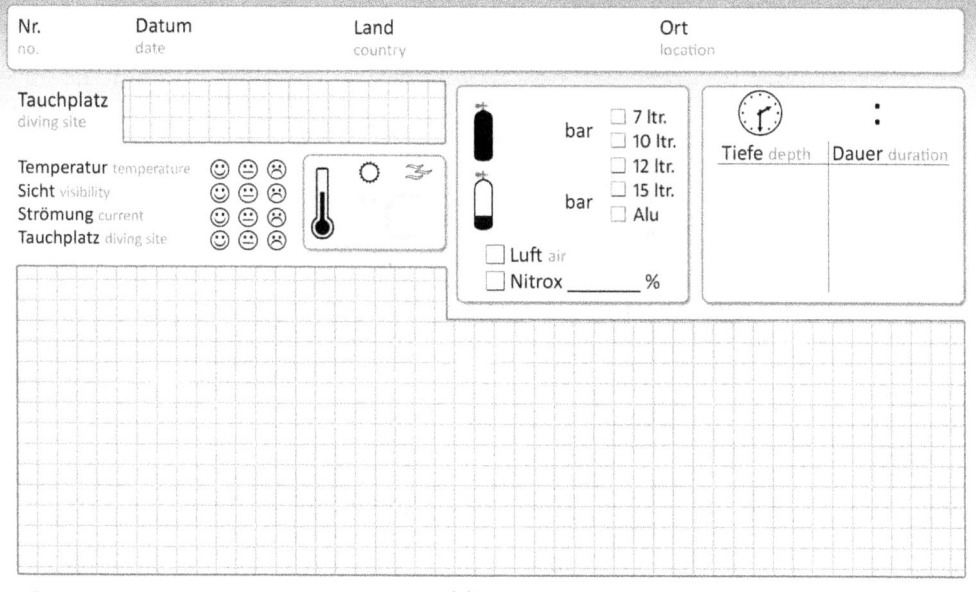

Nr. no.	Datum date	Land country		Ort location		

Tauchplatz diving site

Temperatur temperature ☺ ☻ ☹
Sicht visibility ☺ ☻ ☹
Strömung current ☺ ☻ ☹
Tauchplatz diving site ☺ ☻ ☹

bar
bar

☐ 7 ltr.
☐ 10 ltr.
☐ 12 ltr.
☐ 15 ltr.
☐ Alu

☐ Luft air
☐ Nitrox _____ %

Tiefe depth | Dauer duration

Instructor   **Buddies**
Signature:

No.:

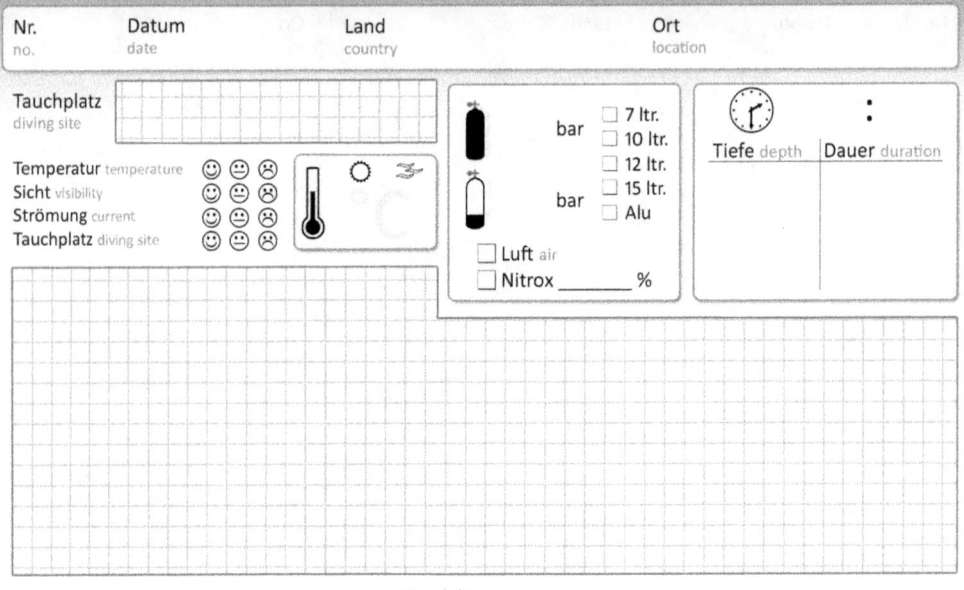

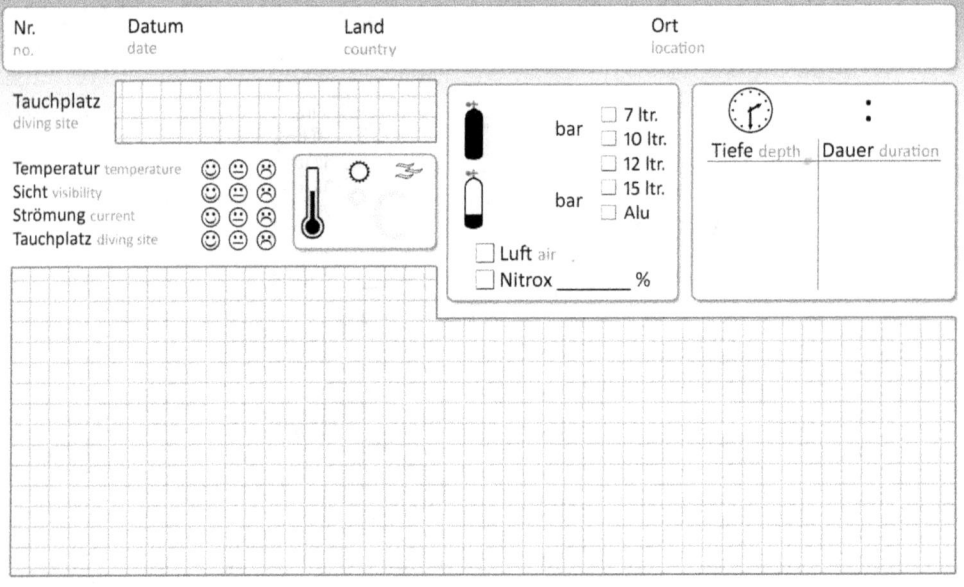

Nr. no.	Datum date	Land country		Ort location	

Tauchplatz diving site

Temperatur temperature ☺ 😐 ☹
Sicht visibility ☺ 😐 ☹
Strömung current ☺ 😐 ☹
Tauchplatz diving site ☺ 😐 ☹

bar ☐ 7 ltr. ☐ 10 ltr. ☐ 12 ltr.
bar ☐ 15 ltr. ☐ Alu
☐ Luft air
☐ Nitrox _____ %

Tiefe depth | Dauer duration

Instructor **Buddies**
Signature:

No.:

Nr. no.	Datum date	Land country		Ort location	

Tauchplatz diving site

Temperatur temperature ☺ 😐 ☹
Sicht visibility ☺ 😐 ☹
Strömung current ☺ 😐 ☹
Tauchplatz diving site ☺ 😐 ☹

bar ☐ 7 ltr. ☐ 10 ltr. ☐ 12 ltr.
bar ☐ 15 ltr. ☐ Alu
☐ Luft air
☐ Nitrox _____ %

Tiefe depth | Dauer duration

Instructor **Buddies**
Signature:

No.:

Nr. no.	Datum date	Land country		Ort location	

Tauchplatz diving site

Temperatur temperature ☺ ☻ ☹
Sicht visibility ☺ ☻ ☹
Strömung current ☺ ☻ ☹
Tauchplatz diving site ☺ ☻ ☹

bar
bar

☐ 7 ltr.
☐ 10 ltr.
☐ 12 ltr.
☐ 15 ltr.
☐ Alu

☐ Luft air
☐ Nitrox _____ %

Tiefe depth | **Dauer** duration

Instructor
Signature:

Buddies

No.:

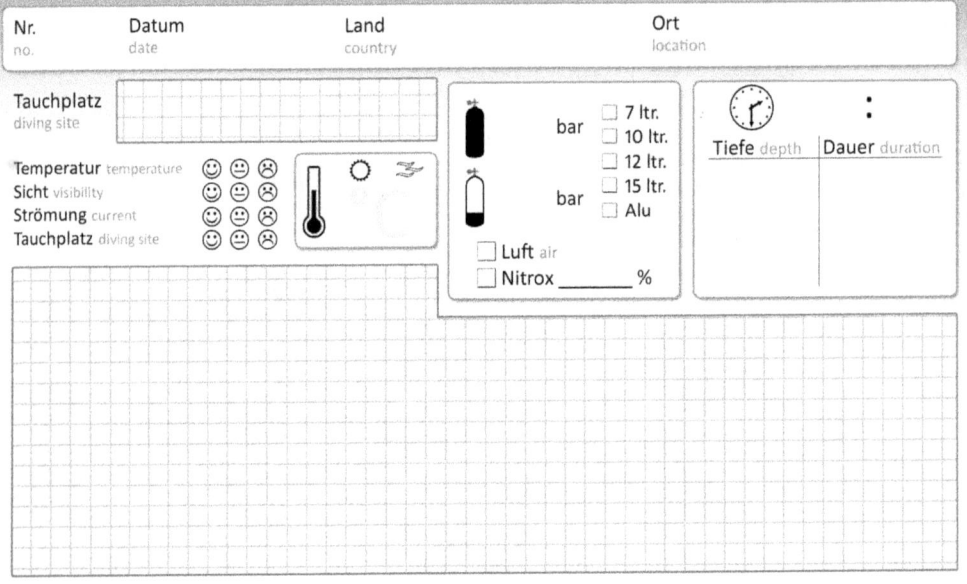

Nr. no.	Datum date	Land country		Ort location	

Tauchplatz diving site

Temperatur temperature ☺ ☻ ☹
Sicht visibility ☺ ☻ ☹
Strömung current ☺ ☻ ☹
Tauchplatz diving site ☺ ☻ ☹

bar
bar

☐ 7 ltr.
☐ 10 ltr.
☐ 12 ltr.
☐ 15 ltr.
☐ Alu

☐ Luft air
☐ Nitrox _____ %

Tiefe depth | **Dauer** duration

Instructor
Signature:

Buddies

No.:

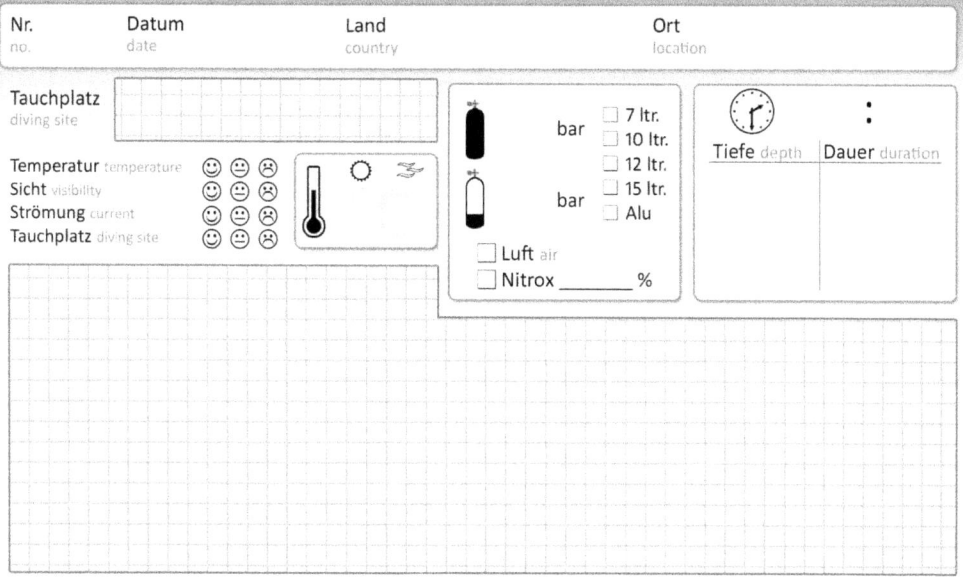

Instructor   Buddies
Signature:

No.:

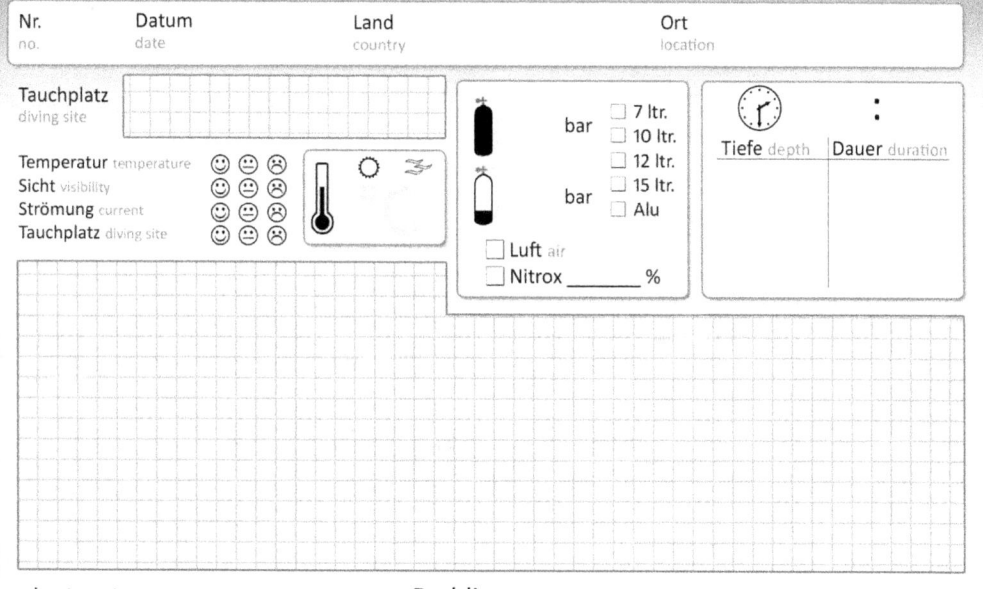

Instructor   Buddies
Signature:

No.:

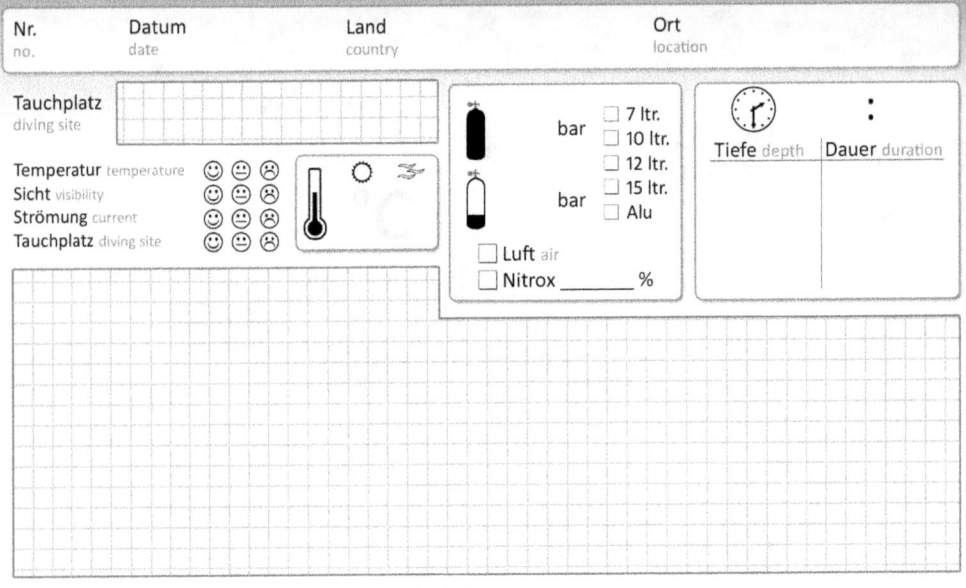

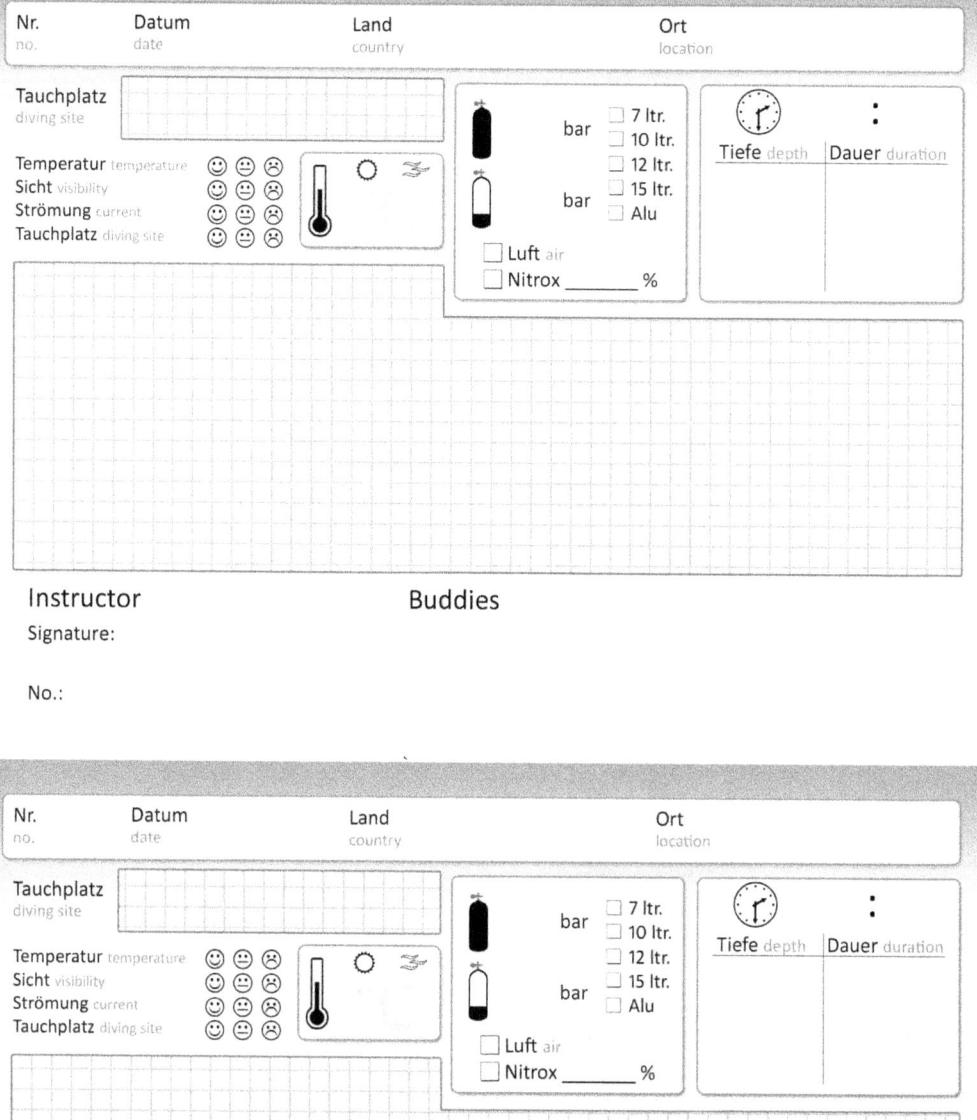

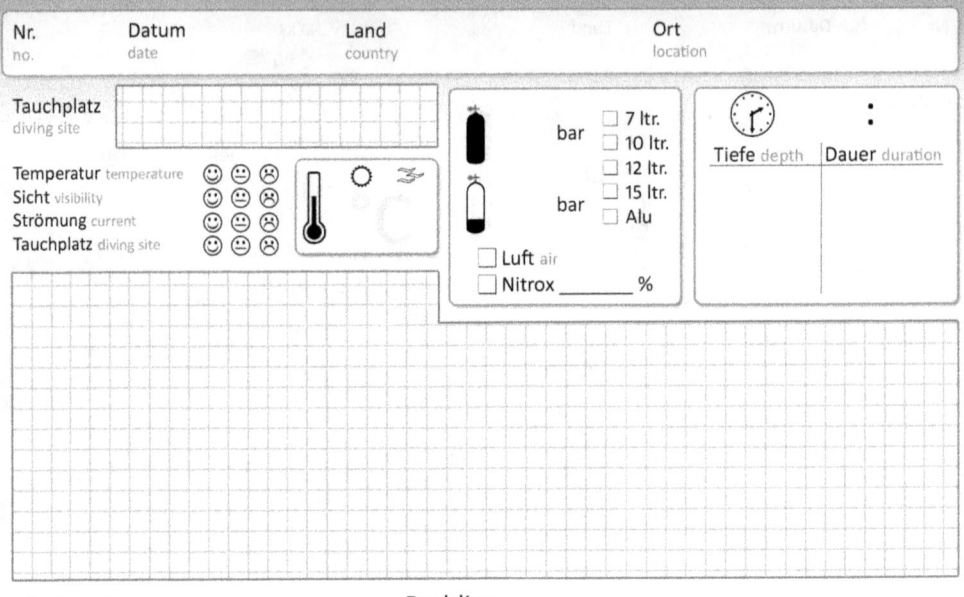

Instructor   Buddies

Signature:

No.:

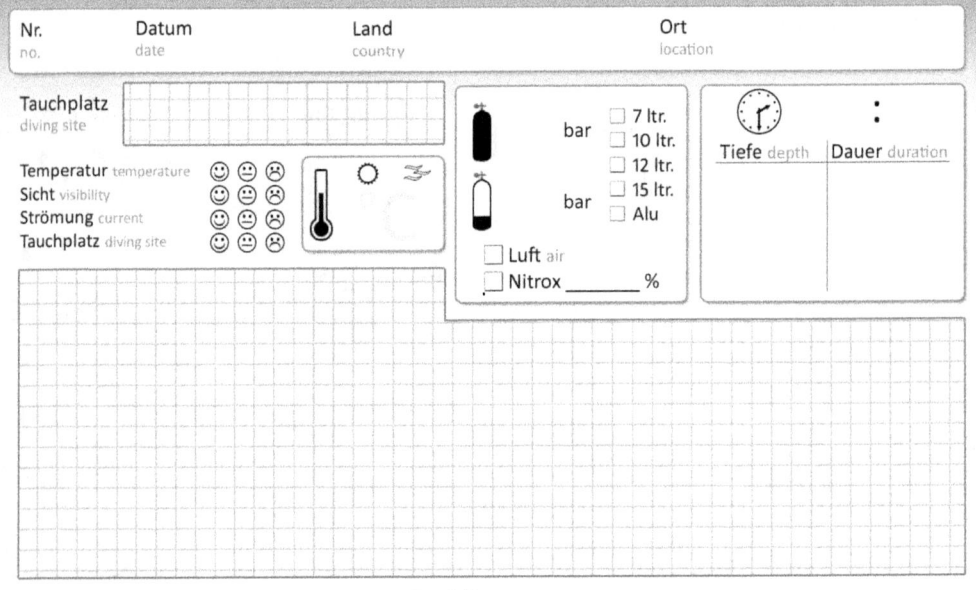

Instructor   Buddies

Signature:

No.:

Nr. no. | Datum date | Land country | Ort location

Tauchplatz diving site

Temperatur temperature ☺ 😐 ☹
Sicht visibility ☺ 😐 ☹
Strömung current ☺ 😐 ☹
Tauchplatz diving site ☺ 😐 ☹

bar
bar

☐ 7 ltr.
☐ 10 ltr.
☐ 12 ltr.
☐ 15 ltr.
☐ Alu

☐ Luft air
☐ Nitrox ________ %

:

Tiefe depth | Dauer duration

Instructor

Signature:

No.:

Buddies

Nr. no. | Datum date | Land country | Ort location

Tauchplatz diving site

Temperatur temperature ☺ 😐 ☹
Sicht visibility ☺ 😐 ☹
Strömung current ☺ 😐 ☹
Tauchplatz diving site ☺ 😐 ☹

bar
bar

☐ 7 ltr.
☐ 10 ltr.
☐ 12 ltr.
☐ 15 ltr.
☐ Alu

☐ Luft air
☐ Nitrox ________ %

:

Tiefe depth | Dauer duration

Instructor

Signature:

No.:

Buddies

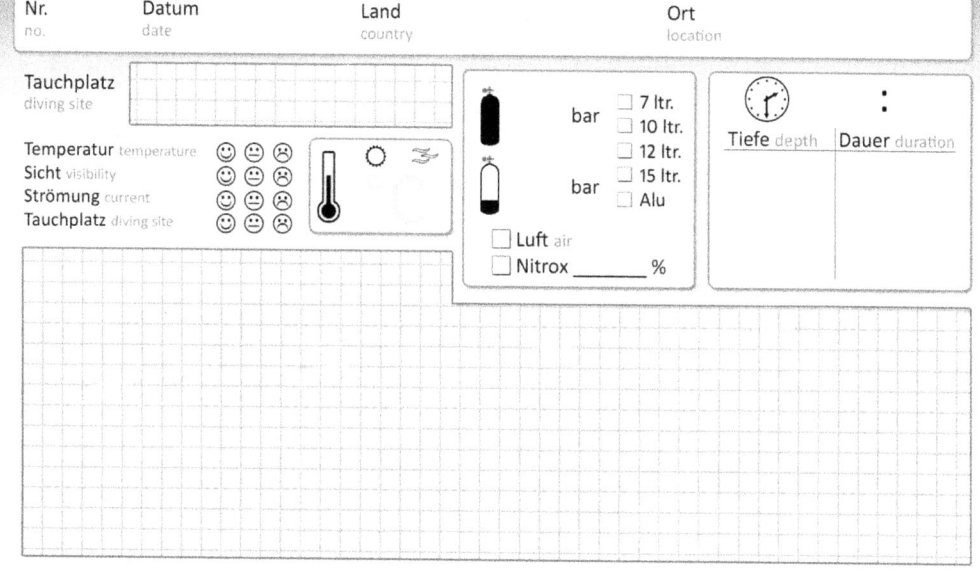

Nr. no.	Datum date	Land country		Ort location	

Tauchplatz diving site

Temperatur temperature
Sicht visibility
Strömung current
Tauchplatz diving site

bar
☐ 7 ltr.
☐ 10 ltr.
☐ 12 ltr.
☐ 15 ltr.
☐ Alu

bar

☐ Luft air
☐ Nitrox _____ %

Tiefe depth | Dauer duration

Instructor   Buddies

Signature:

No.:

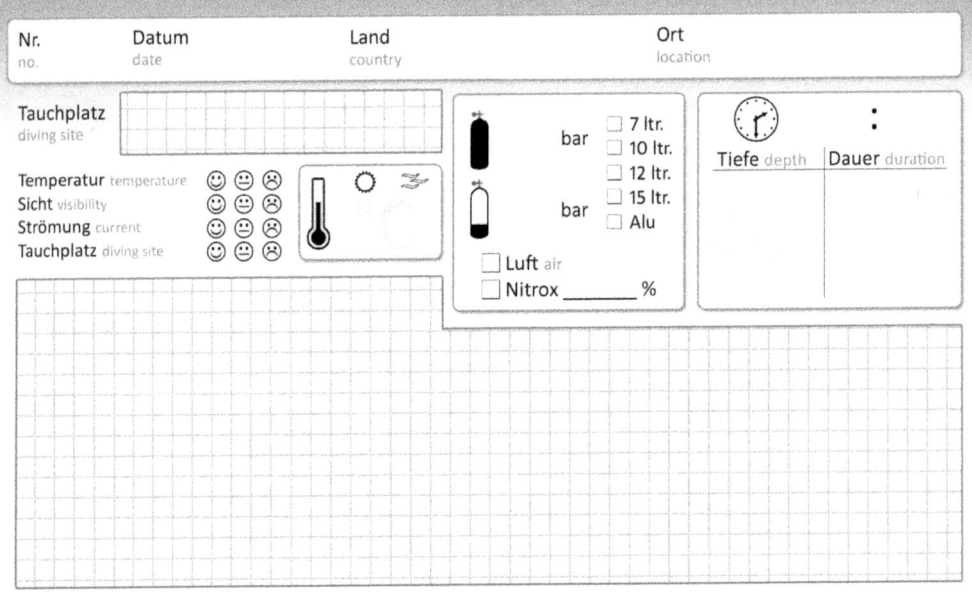

Nr. no.	Datum date	Land country		Ort location	

Tauchplatz diving site

Temperatur temperature
Sicht visibility
Strömung current
Tauchplatz diving site

bar
☐ 7 ltr.
☐ 10 ltr.
☐ 12 ltr.
☐ 15 ltr.
☐ Alu

bar

☐ Luft air
☐ Nitrox _____ %

Tiefe depth | Dauer duration

Instructor   Buddies

Signature:

No.:

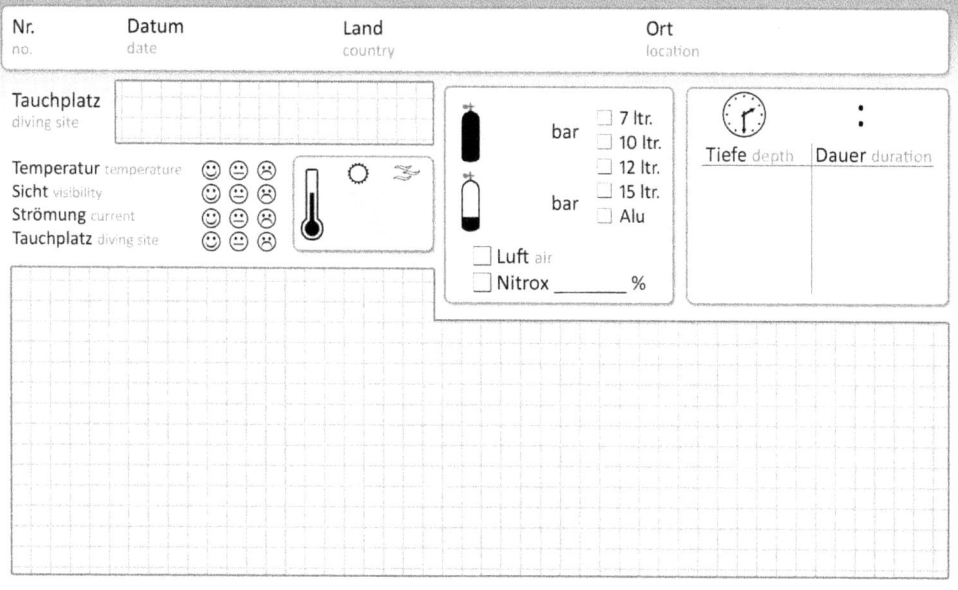

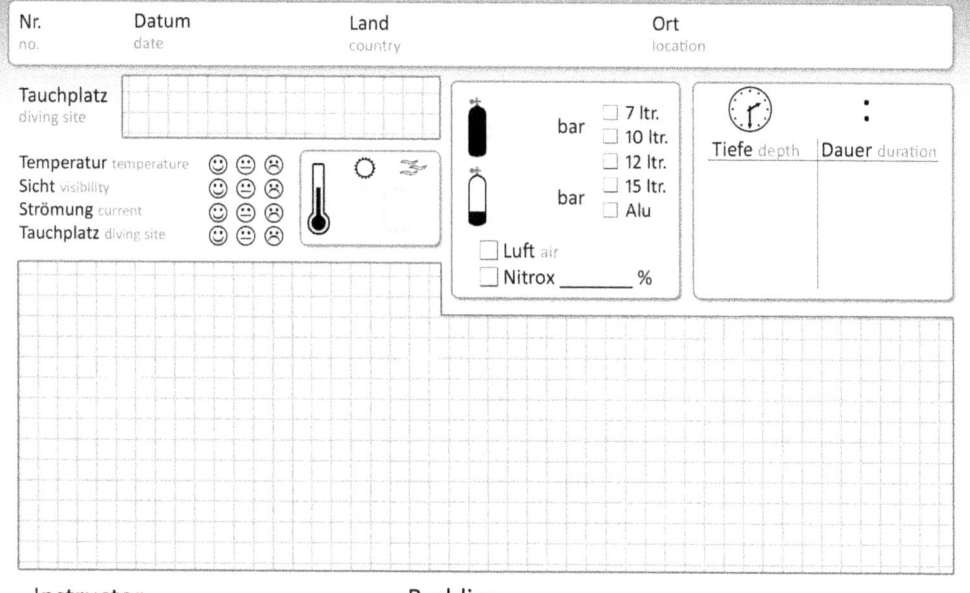

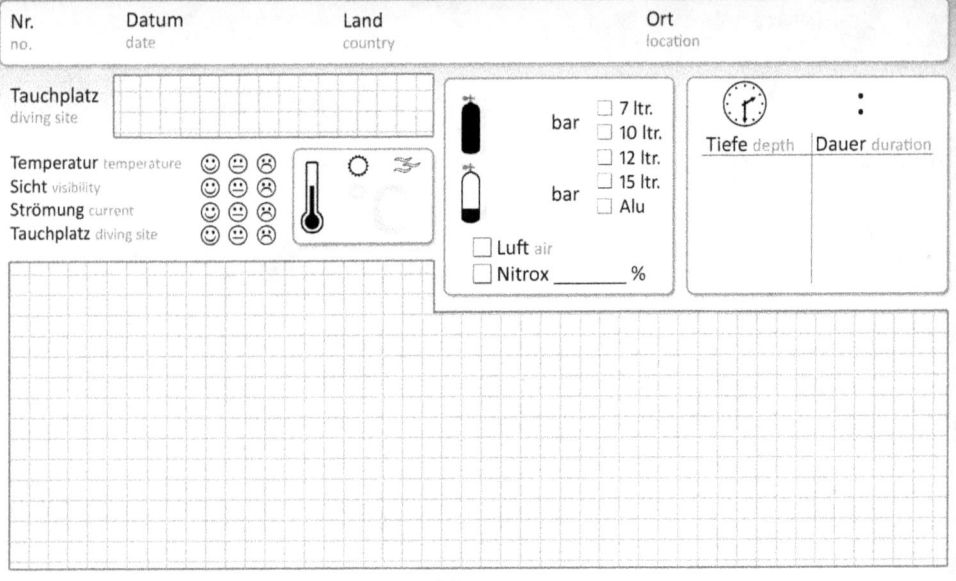

Instructor   Buddies

Signature:

No.:

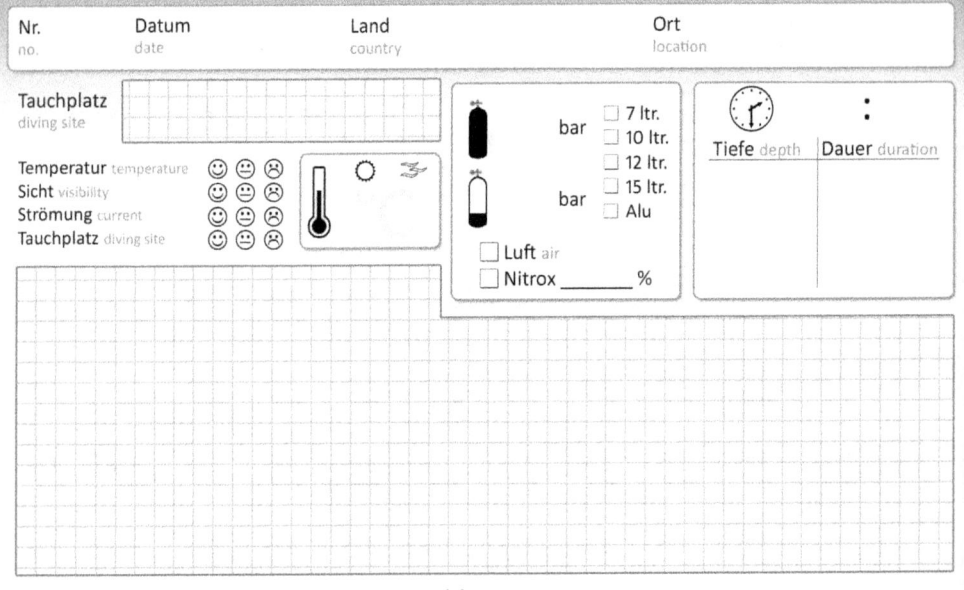

Instructor   Buddies

Signature:

No.:

Nr. no.	Datum date	Land country		Ort location	

Tauchplatz diving site

Temperatur temperature ☺ 😐 ☹
Sicht visibility ☺ 😐 ☹
Strömung current ☺ 😐 ☹
Tauchplatz diving site ☺ 😐 ☹

bar ☐ 7 ltr. ☐ 10 ltr. ☐ 12 ltr.
bar ☐ 15 ltr. ☐ Alu
☐ Luft air
☐ Nitrox _____ %

Tiefe depth | **Dauer** duration

Instructor   Buddies
Signature:

No.:

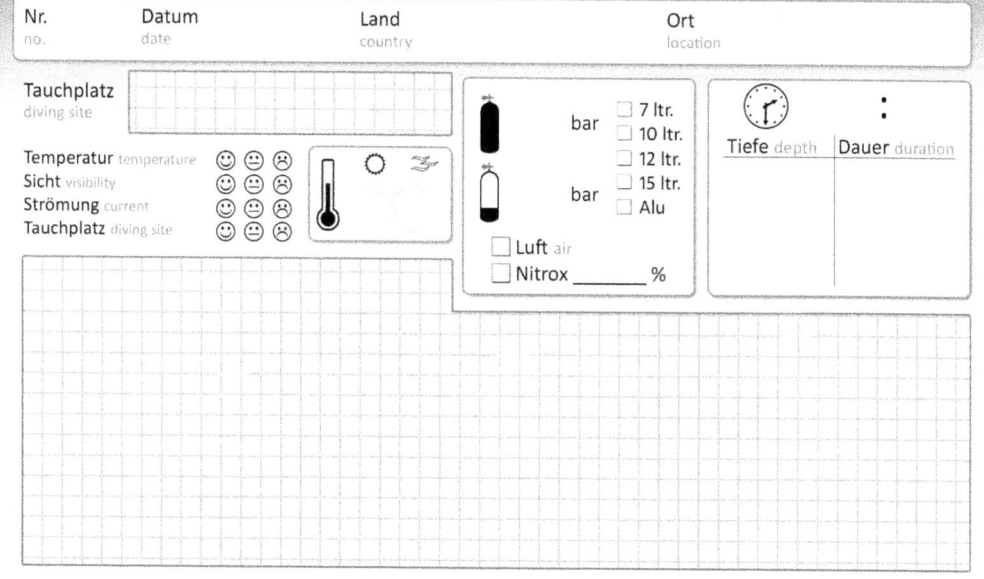

Instructor   Buddies
Signature:

No.:

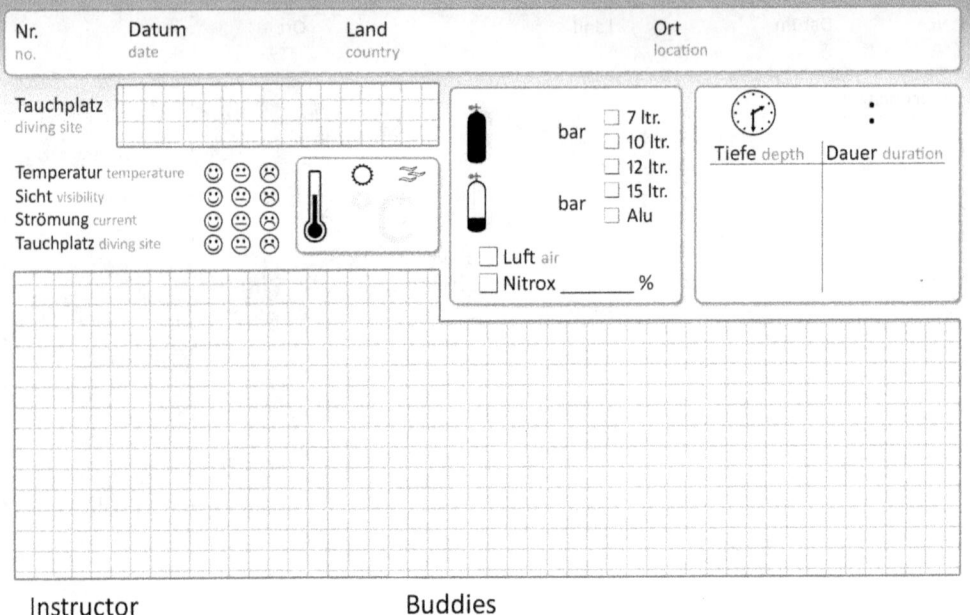

Nr. no.	Datum date	Land country	Ort location

Tauchplatz diving site

Temperatur temperature
Sicht visibility
Strömung current
Tauchplatz diving site

☐ 7 ltr.
☐ 10 ltr.
☐ 12 ltr.
☐ 15 ltr.
☐ Alu

bar
bar

☐ Luft air
☐ Nitrox _____ %

Tiefe depth | Dauer duration

Instructor   Buddies
Signature:

No.:

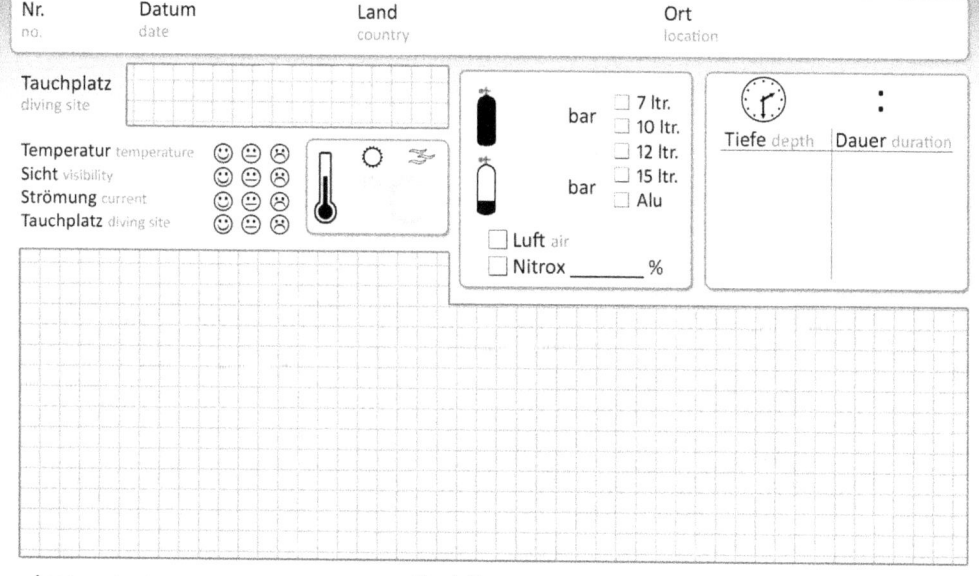

Nr. no.	Datum date	Land country	Ort location

Tauchplatz diving site

Temperatur temperature
Sicht visibility
Strömung current
Tauchplatz diving site

☐ 7 ltr.
☐ 10 ltr.
☐ 12 ltr.
☐ 15 ltr.
☐ Alu

bar
bar

☐ Luft air
☐ Nitrox _____ %

Tiefe depth | Dauer duration

Instructor   Buddies
Signature:

No.:

Nr. no.	Datum date	Land country		Ort location	

Tauchplatz diving site

Temperatur temperature ☺ 😐 ☹
Sicht visibility ☺ 😐 ☹
Strömung current ☺ 😐 ☹
Tauchplatz diving site ☺ 😐 ☹

bar
☐ 7 ltr.
☐ 10 ltr.
☐ 12 ltr.
☐ 15 ltr.
☐ Alu
bar

☐ Luft air
☐ Nitrox _____ %

Tiefe depth | **Dauer** duration

Instructor   **Buddies**
Signature:

No.:

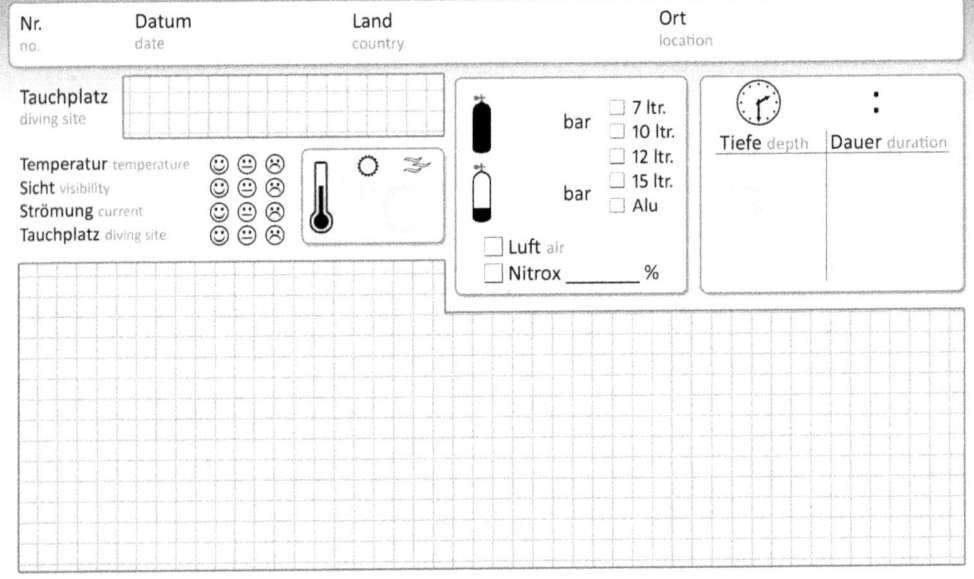

Nr. no.	Datum date	Land country		Ort location	

Tauchplatz diving site

Temperatur temperature ☺ 😐 ☹
Sicht visibility ☺ 😐 ☹
Strömung current ☺ 😐 ☹
Tauchplatz diving site ☺ 😐 ☹

bar
☐ 7 ltr.
☐ 10 ltr.
☐ 12 ltr.
☐ 15 ltr.
☐ Alu
bar

☐ Luft air
☐ Nitrox _____ %

Tiefe depth | **Dauer** duration

Instructor   **Buddies**
Signature:

No.:

Nr. no.	Datum date	Land country	Ort location

Tauchplatz diving site

Temperatur temperature ☺ 😐 ☹
Sicht visibility ☺ 😐 ☹
Strömung current ☺ 😐 ☹
Tauchplatz diving site ☺ 😐 ☹

bar ☐ 7 ltr.
☐ 10 ltr.
☐ 12 ltr.
bar ☐ 15 ltr.
☐ Alu

☐ Luft air
☐ Nitrox _____ %

Tiefe depth | **Dauer** duration

Instructor
Signature:

Buddies

No.:

Nr. no.	Datum date	Land country	Ort location

Tauchplatz diving site

Temperatur temperature ☺ 😐 ☹
Sicht visibility ☺ 😐 ☹
Strömung current ☺ 😐 ☹
Tauchplatz diving site ☺ 😐 ☹

bar ☐ 7 ltr.
☐ 10 ltr.
☐ 12 ltr.
bar ☐ 15 ltr.
☐ Alu

☐ Luft air
☐ Nitrox _____ %

Tiefe depth | **Dauer** duration

Instructor
Signature:

Buddies

No.:

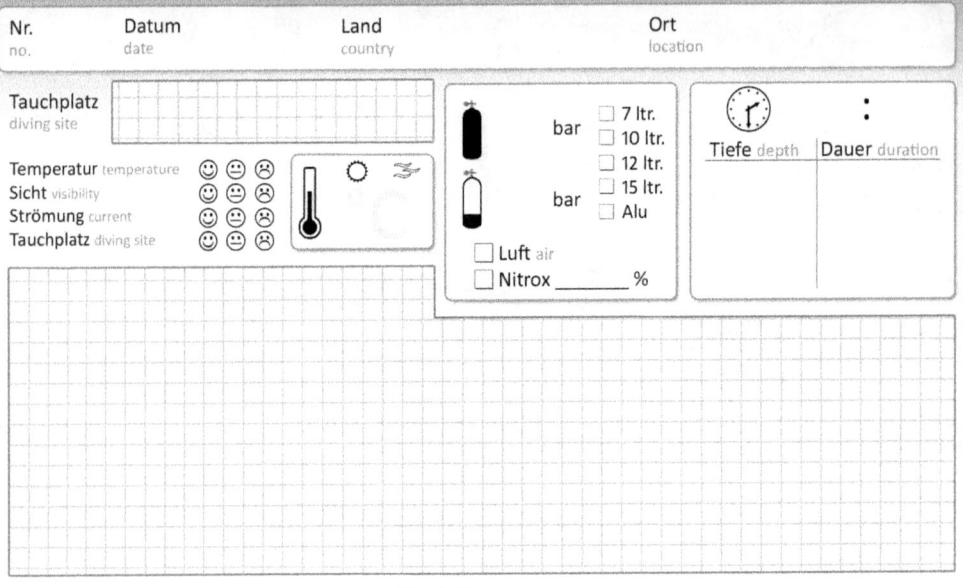

Instructor   Buddies

Signature:

No.:

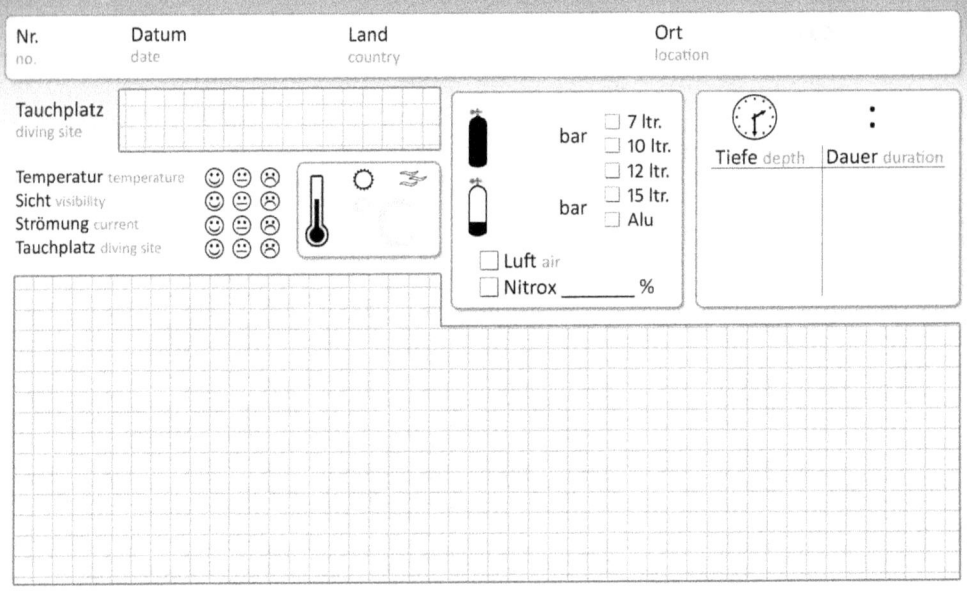

Instructor   Buddies

Signature:

No.:

Nr. no. | Datum date | Land country | Ort location

Tauchplatz diving site

Temperatur temperature
Sicht visibility
Strömung current
Tauchplatz diving site

bar
bar

7 ltr.
10 ltr.
12 ltr.
15 ltr.
Alu

Luft air
Nitrox ________ %

:

Tiefe depth | Dauer duration

Instructor

Buddies

Signature:

No.:

Nr. no. | Datum date | Land country | Ort location

Tauchplatz diving site

Temperatur temperature
Sicht visibility
Strömung current
Tauchplatz diving site

bar
bar

7 ltr.
10 ltr.
12 ltr.
15 ltr.
Alu

Luft air
Nitrox ________ %

:

Tiefe depth | Dauer duration

Instructor

Buddies

Signature:

No.:

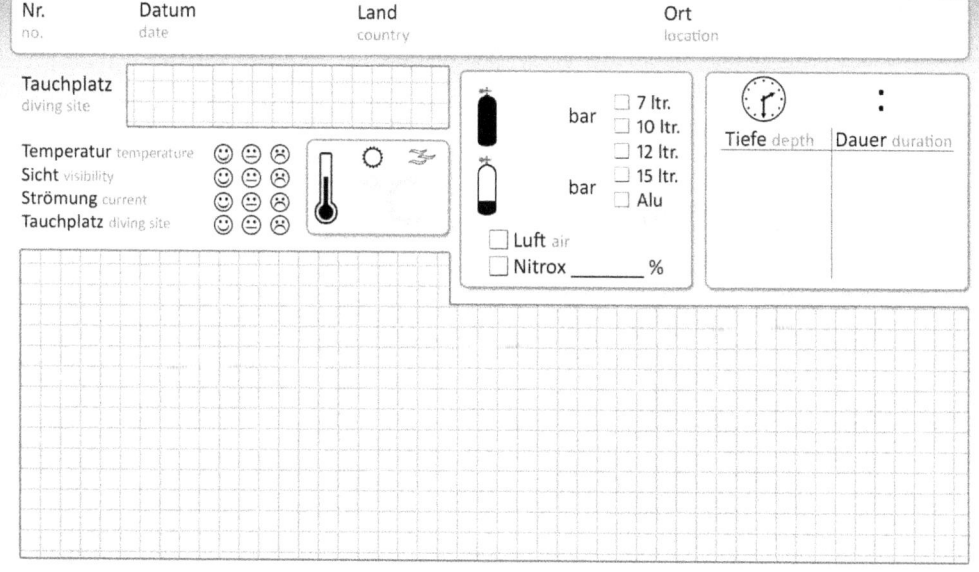

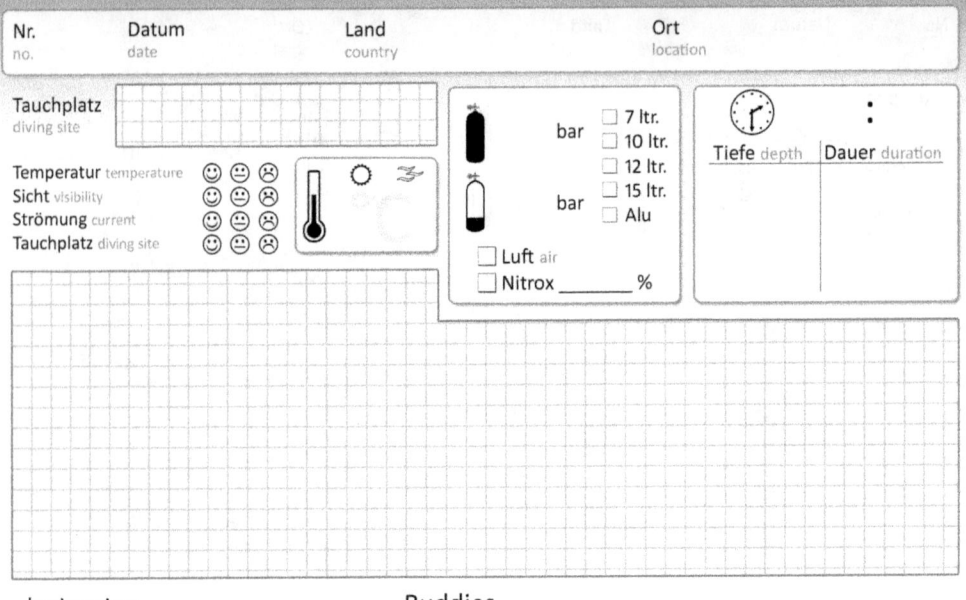

Instructor   Buddies
Signature:

No.:

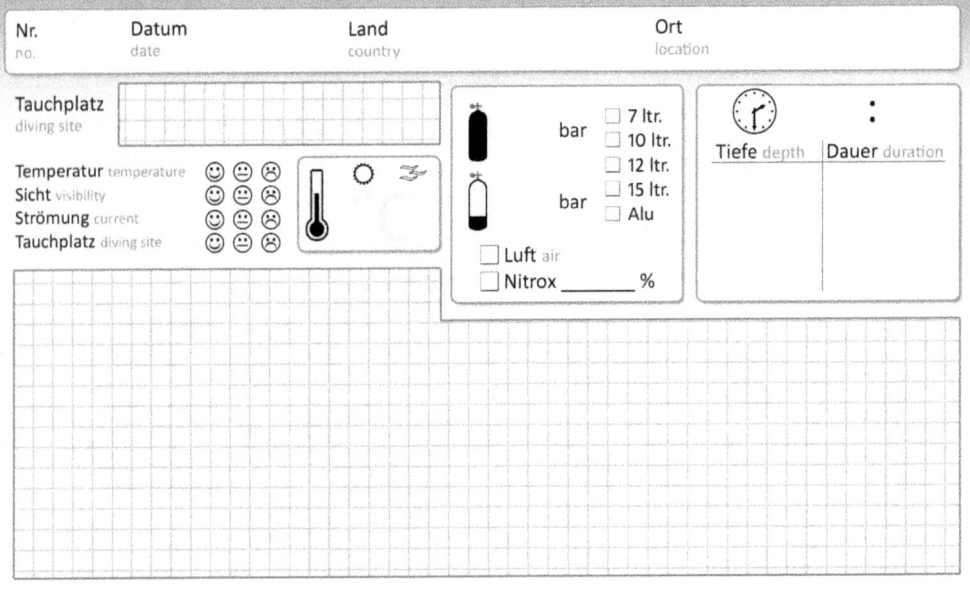

Instructor   Buddies
Signature:

No.:

Nr. no.	Datum date	Land country	Ort location

Tauchplatz diving site

Temperatur temperature
Sicht visibility
Strömung current
Tauchplatz diving site

bar
bar

- [ ] 7 ltr.
- [ ] 10 ltr.
- [ ] 12 ltr.
- [ ] 15 ltr.
- [ ] Alu

- [ ] Luft air
- [ ] Nitrox _____ %

Tiefe depth	Dauer duration

Instructor
Signature:

Buddies

No.:

Nr. no.	Datum date	Land country	Ort location

Tauchplatz diving site

Temperatur temperature
Sicht visibility
Strömung current
Tauchplatz diving site

bar
bar

- [ ] 7 ltr.
- [ ] 10 ltr.
- [ ] 12 ltr.
- [ ] 15 ltr.
- [ ] Alu

- [ ] Luft air
- [ ] Nitrox _____ %

Tiefe depth	Dauer duration

Instructor
Signature:

Buddies

No.:

Nr. no.	Datum date	Land country		Ort location	

Tauchplatz diving site

Temperatur temperature ☺ ☻ ☹
Sicht visibility ☺ ☻ ☹
Strömung current ☺ ☻ ☹
Tauchplatz diving site ☺ ☻ ☹

bar ☐ 7 ltr.
     ☐ 10 ltr.
     ☐ 12 ltr.
bar ☐ 15 ltr.
     ☐ Alu

☐ Luft air
☐ Nitrox _____ %

Tiefe depth	Dauer duration

Instructor

Buddies

Signature:

No.:

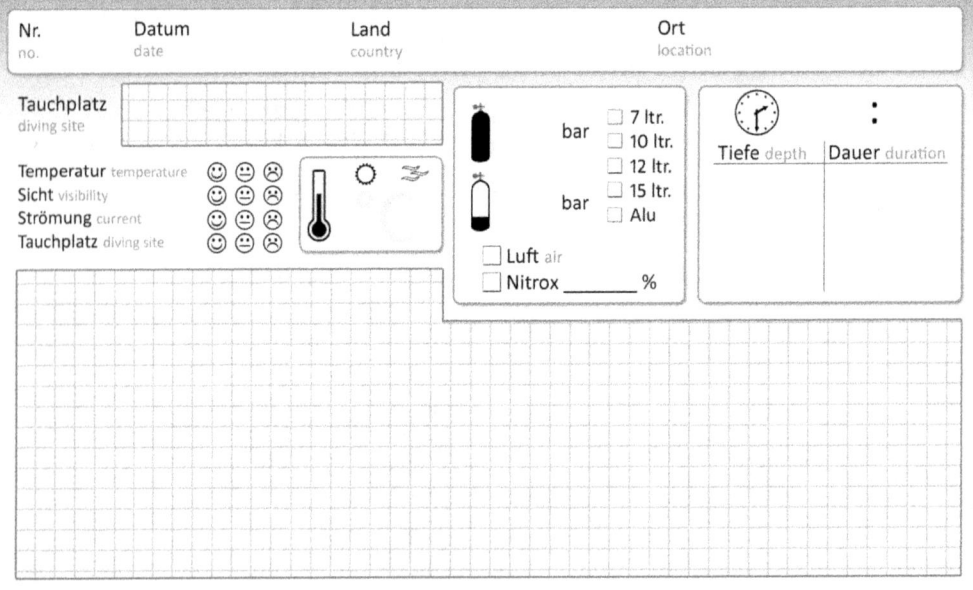

Nr. no.	Datum date	Land country		Ort location	

Tauchplatz diving site

Temperatur temperature ☺ ☻ ☹
Sicht visibility ☺ ☻ ☹
Strömung current ☺ ☻ ☹
Tauchplatz diving site ☺ ☻ ☹

bar ☐ 7 ltr.
     ☐ 10 ltr.
     ☐ 12 ltr.
bar ☐ 15 ltr.
     ☐ Alu

☐ Luft air
☐ Nitrox _____ %

Tiefe depth	Dauer duration

Instructor

Buddies

Signature:

No.:

| Nr. no. | Datum date | Land country | Ort location |

Tauchplatz diving site

Temperatur temperature ☺ 😐 ☹
Sicht visibility ☺ 😐 ☹
Strömung current ☺ 😐 ☹
Tauchplatz diving site ☺ 😐 ☹

___ bar
___ bar

☐ 7 ltr.
☐ 10 ltr.
☐ 12 ltr.
☐ 15 ltr.
☐ Alu
☐ Luft air
☐ Nitrox ___ %

| Tiefe depth | Dauer duration |

Instructor
Signature:

Buddies

No.:

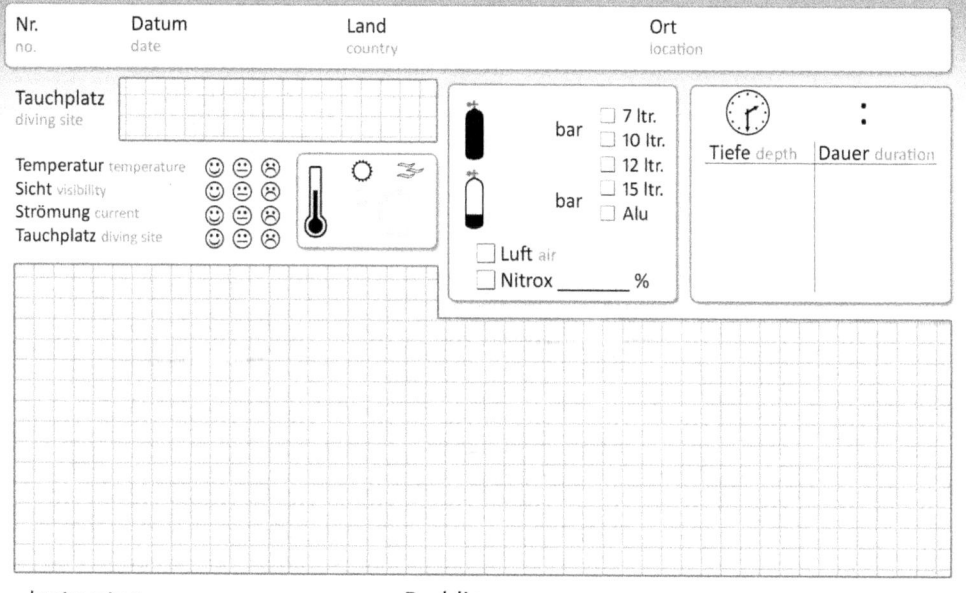

| Nr. no. | Datum date | Land country | Ort location |

Tauchplatz diving site

Temperatur temperature ☺ 😐 ☹
Sicht visibility ☺ 😐 ☹
Strömung current ☺ 😐 ☹
Tauchplatz diving site ☺ 😐 ☹

___ bar
___ bar

☐ 7 ltr.
☐ 10 ltr.
☐ 12 ltr.
☐ 15 ltr.
☐ Alu
☐ Luft air
☐ Nitrox ___ %

| Tiefe depth | Dauer duration |

Instructor
Signature:

Buddies

No.:

Nr. no.	Datum date	Land country	Ort location

Tauchplatz diving site

Temperatur temperature
Sicht visibility
Strömung current
Tauchplatz diving site

Tiefe depth	Dauer duration

bar ☐ 7 ltr. ☐ 10 ltr. ☐ 12 ltr. ☐ 15 ltr. ☐ Alu
bar
☐ Luft air
☐ Nitrox _____ %

Instructor
Signature:

Buddies

No.:

Nr. no.	Datum date	Land country	Ort location

Tauchplatz diving site

Temperatur temperature
Sicht visibility
Strömung current
Tauchplatz diving site

Tiefe depth	Dauer duration

bar ☐ 7 ltr. ☐ 10 ltr. ☐ 12 ltr. ☐ 15 ltr. ☐ Alu
bar
☐ Luft air
☐ Nitrox _____ %

Instructor
Signature:

Buddies

No.:

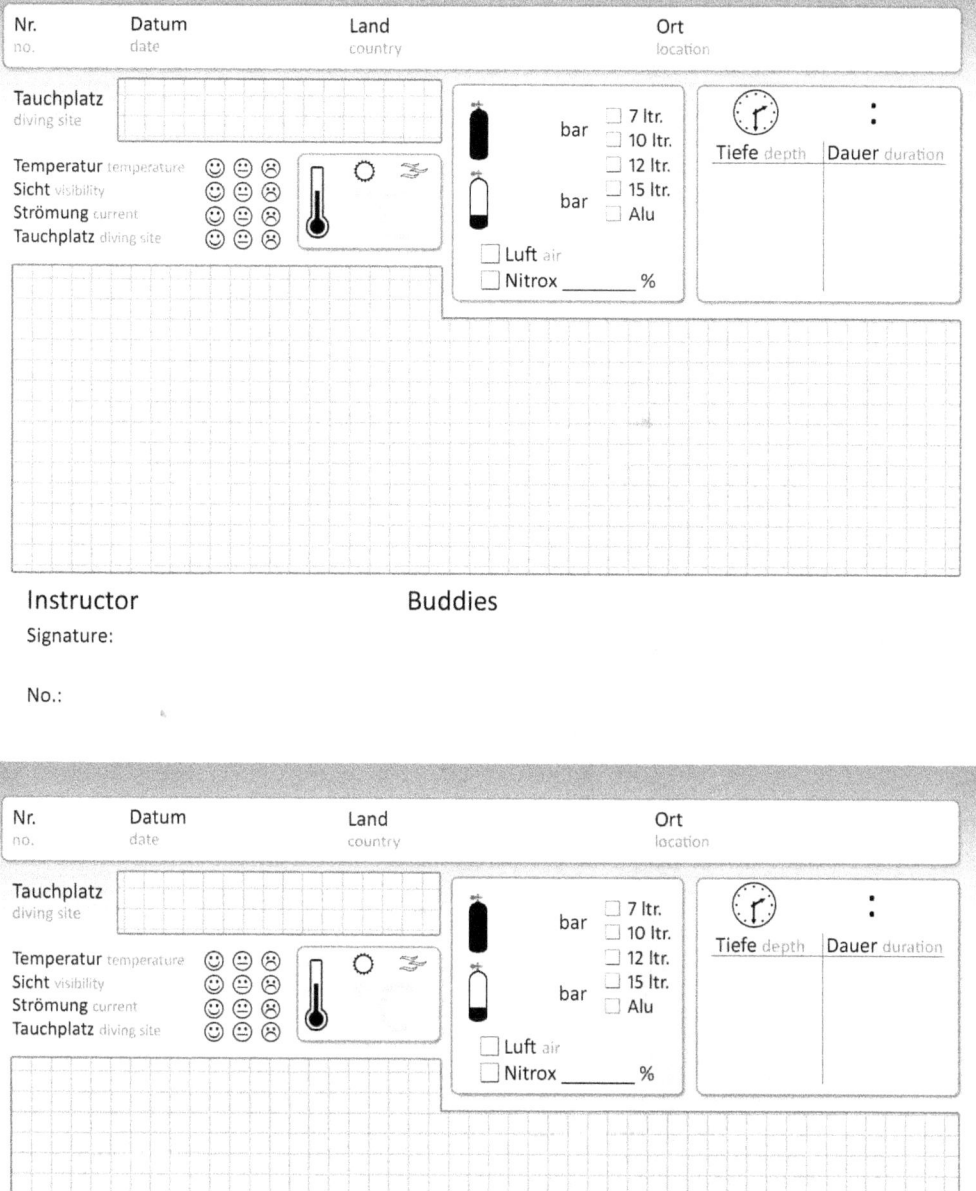

Nr. no.	Datum date	Land country		Ort location	

Tauchplatz diving site

Temperatur temperature 😊 😐 ☹
Sicht visibility 😊 😐 ☹
Strömung current 😊 😐 ☹
Tauchplatz diving site 😊 😐 ☹

bar
☐ 7 ltr.
☐ 10 ltr.
☐ 12 ltr.
☐ 15 ltr.
☐ Alu

bar

☐ Luft air
☐ Nitrox _____ %

Tiefe depth	Dauer duration

Instructor
Signature:

Buddies

No.:

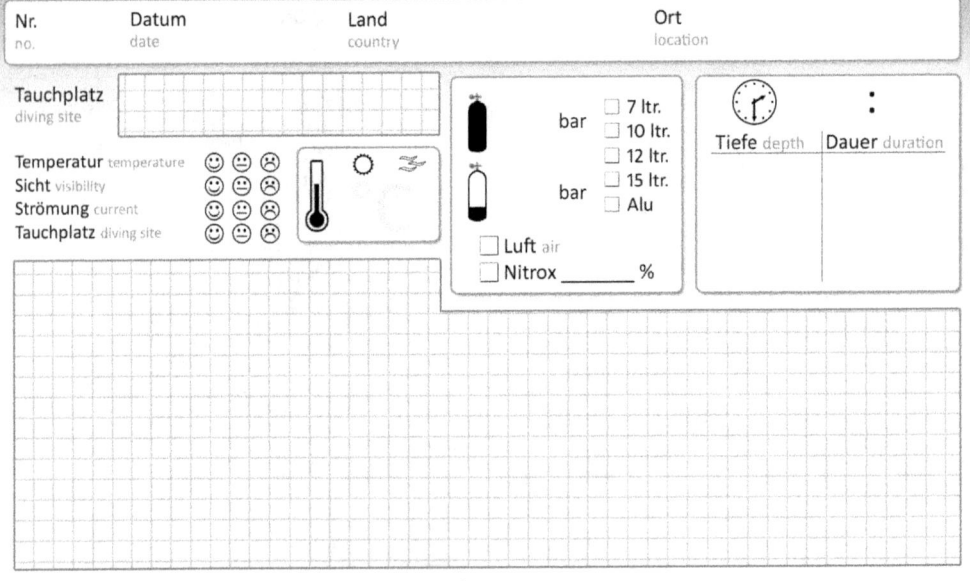

Nr. no.	Datum date	Land country		Ort location	

Tauchplatz diving site

Temperatur temperature 😊 😐 ☹
Sicht visibility 😊 😐 ☹
Strömung current 😊 😐 ☹
Tauchplatz diving site 😊 😐 ☹

bar
☐ 7 ltr.
☐ 10 ltr.
☐ 12 ltr.
☐ 15 ltr.
☐ Alu

bar

☐ Luft air
☐ Nitrox _____ %

Tiefe depth	Dauer duration

Instructor
Signature:

Buddies

No.:

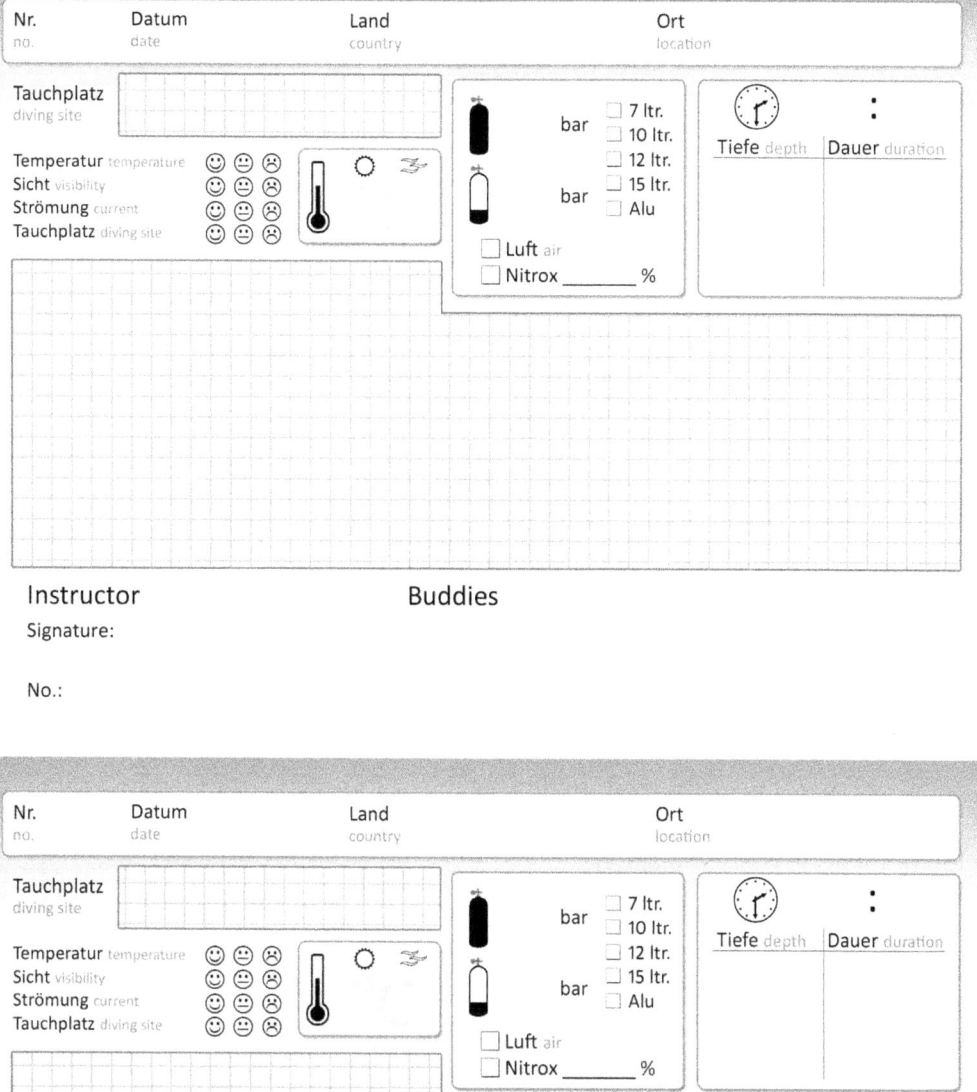

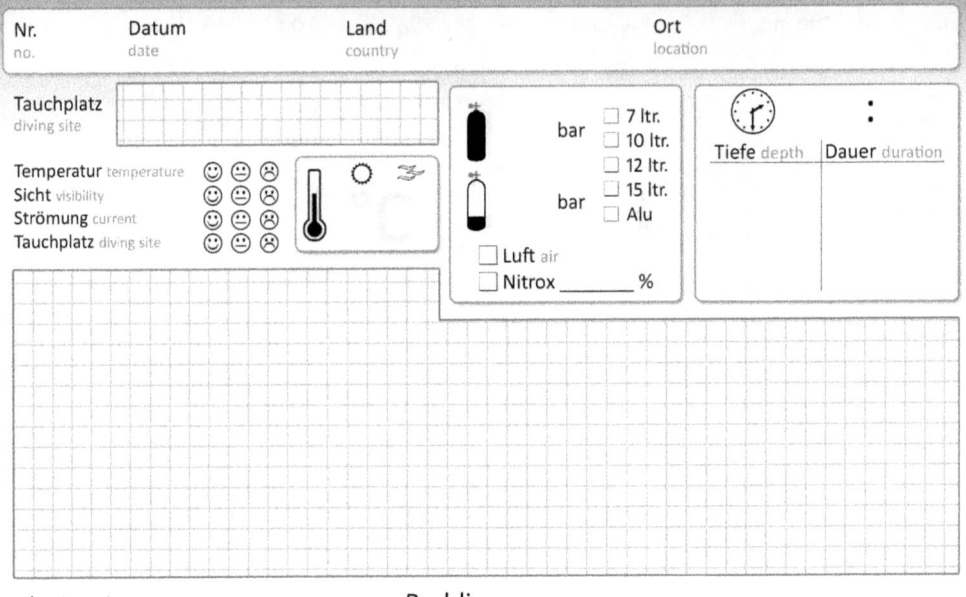

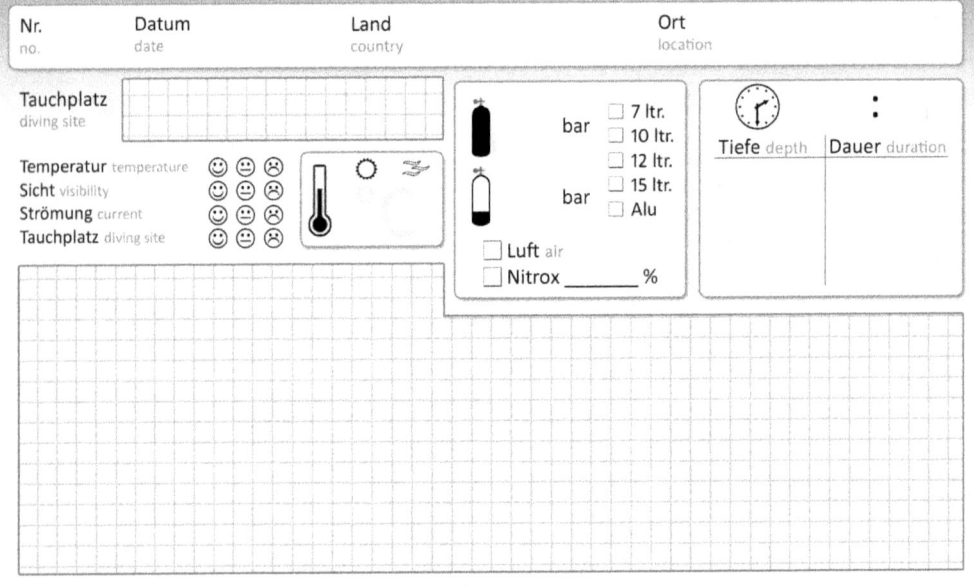

| Nr. no. | Datum date | Land country | Ort location |

Tauchplatz diving site

Temperatur temperature ☺ 😐 ☹
Sicht visibility ☺ 😐 ☹
Strömung current ☺ 😐 ☹
Tauchplatz diving site ☺ 😐 ☹

bar ☐ 7 ltr.
☐ 10 ltr.
bar ☐ 12 ltr.
☐ 15 ltr.
☐ Alu

Tiefe depth | Dauer duration

☐ Luft air
☐ Nitrox _____ %

Instructor   Buddies
Signature:

No.:

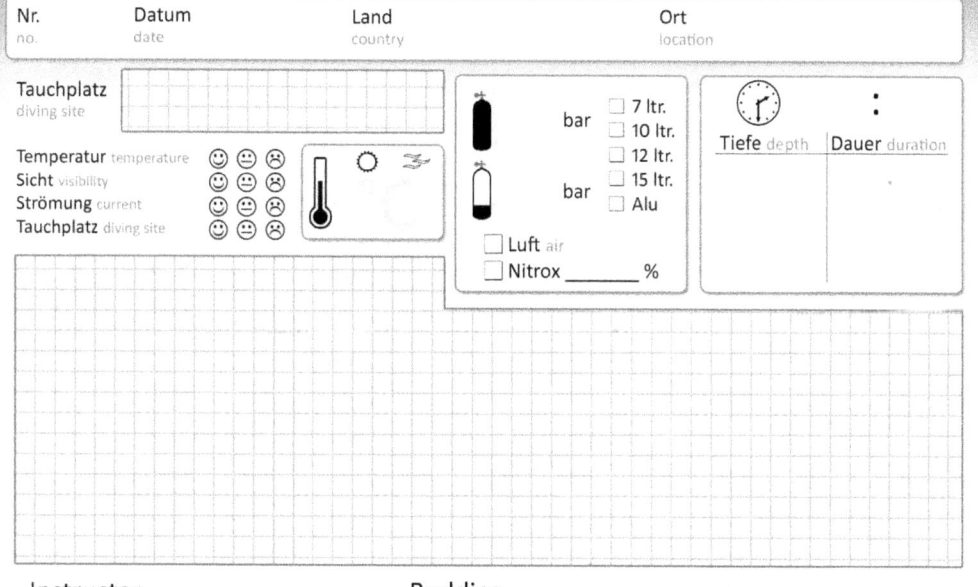

| Nr. no. | Datum date | Land country | Ort location |

Tauchplatz diving site

Temperatur temperature ☺ 😐 ☹
Sicht visibility ☺ 😐 ☹
Strömung current ☺ 😐 ☹
Tauchplatz diving site ☺ 😐 ☹

bar ☐ 7 ltr.
☐ 10 ltr.
bar ☐ 12 ltr.
☐ 15 ltr.
☐ Alu

Tiefe depth | Dauer duration

☐ Luft air
☐ Nitrox _____ %

Instructor   Buddies
Signature:

No.:

Nr. no.	Datum date	Land country		Ort location	

Tauchplatz diving site

Temperatur temperature
Sicht visibility
Strömung current
Tauchplatz diving site

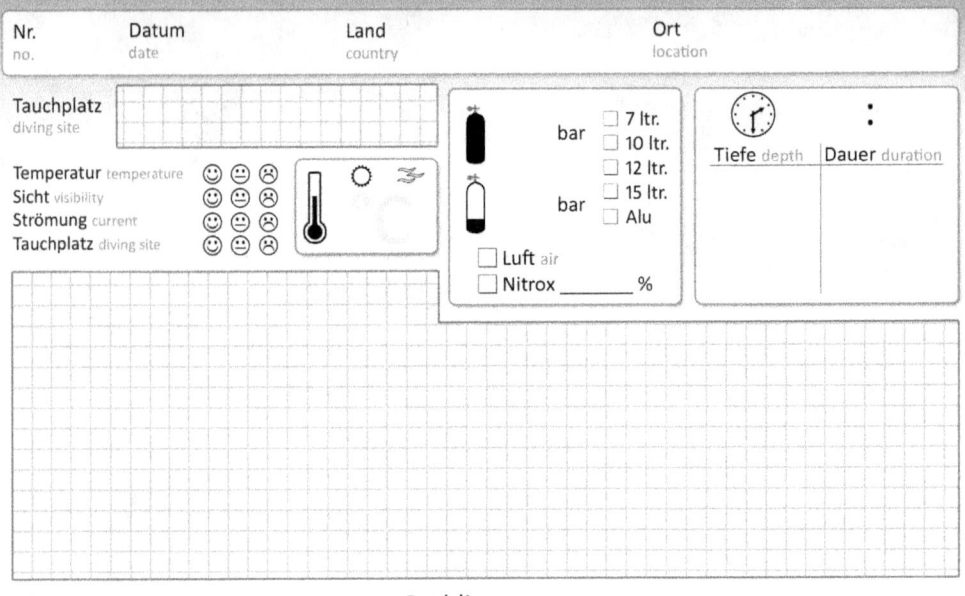

Tiefe depth	Dauer duration

Instructor
Signature:

Buddies

No.:

Nr. no.	Datum date	Land country		Ort location	

Tauchplatz diving site

Temperatur temperature
Sicht visibility
Strömung current
Tauchplatz diving site

Tiefe depth	Dauer duration

Instructor
Signature:

Buddies

No.:

Nr. no.	Datum date	Land country		Ort location	

Tauchplatz diving site

Temperatur temperature ☺ ☺ ☹
Sicht visibility ☺ ☺ ☹
Strömung current ☺ ☺ ☹
Tauchplatz diving site ☺ ☺ ☹

bar ☐ 7 ltr. ☐ 10 ltr. ☐ 12 ltr.
bar ☐ 15 ltr. ☐ Alu
☐ Luft air
☐ Nitrox _____ %

Tiefe depth | Dauer duration

Instructor   **Buddies**
Signature:

No.:

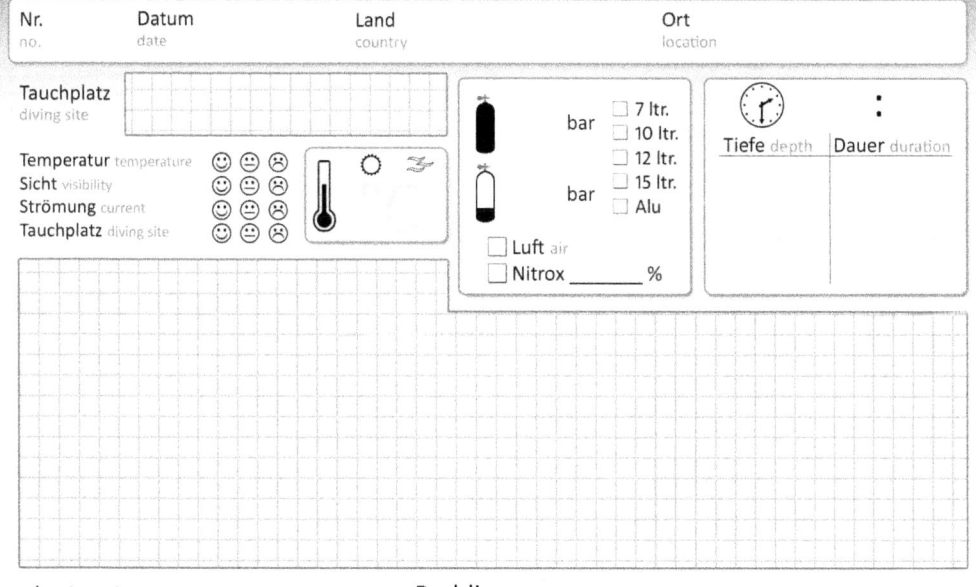

Instructor   **Buddies**
Signature:

No.:

Nr. no.	Datum date	Land country		Ort location		

Tauchplatz diving site

Temperatur temperature ☺ 😐 ☹
Sicht visibility ☺ 😐 ☹
Strömung current ☺ 😐 ☹
Tauchplatz diving site ☺ 😐 ☹

bar ☐ 7 ltr. ☐ 10 ltr. ☐ 12 ltr.
bar ☐ 15 ltr. ☐ Alu

☐ Luft air
☐ Nitrox _____ %

Tiefe depth	Dauer duration

Instructor   Buddies
Signature:

No.:

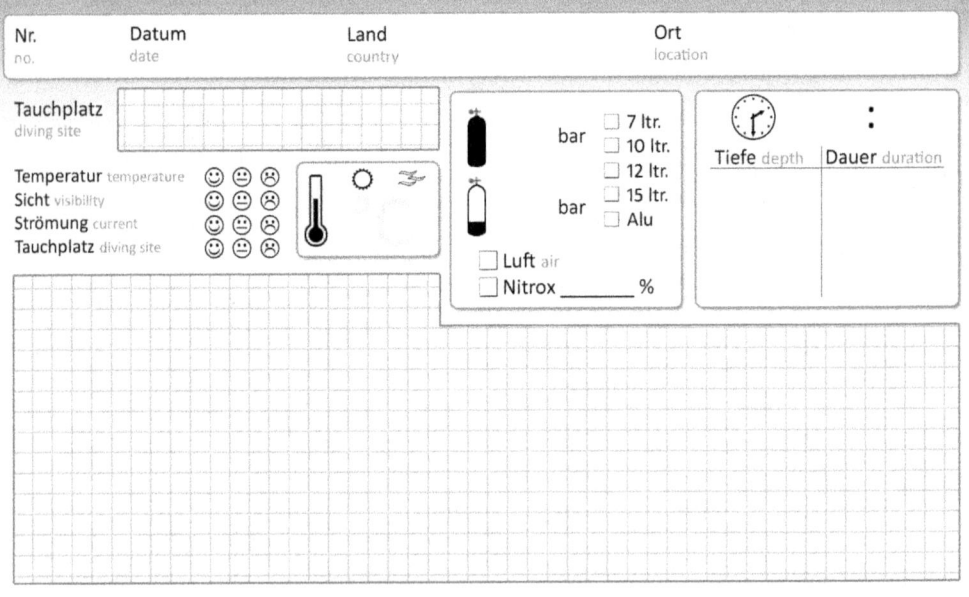

Nr. no.	Datum date	Land country		Ort location		

Tauchplatz diving site

Temperatur temperature ☺ 😐 ☹
Sicht visibility ☺ 😐 ☹
Strömung current ☺ 😐 ☹
Tauchplatz diving site ☺ 😐 ☹

bar ☐ 7 ltr. ☐ 10 ltr. ☐ 12 ltr.
bar ☐ 15 ltr. ☐ Alu

☐ Luft air
☐ Nitrox _____ %

Tiefe depth	Dauer duration

Instructor   Buddies
Signature:

No.:

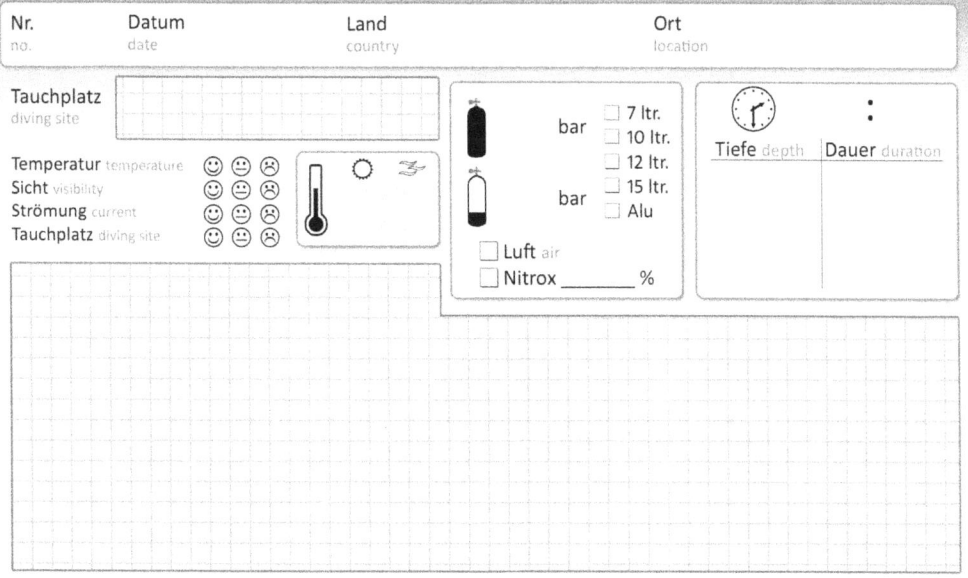

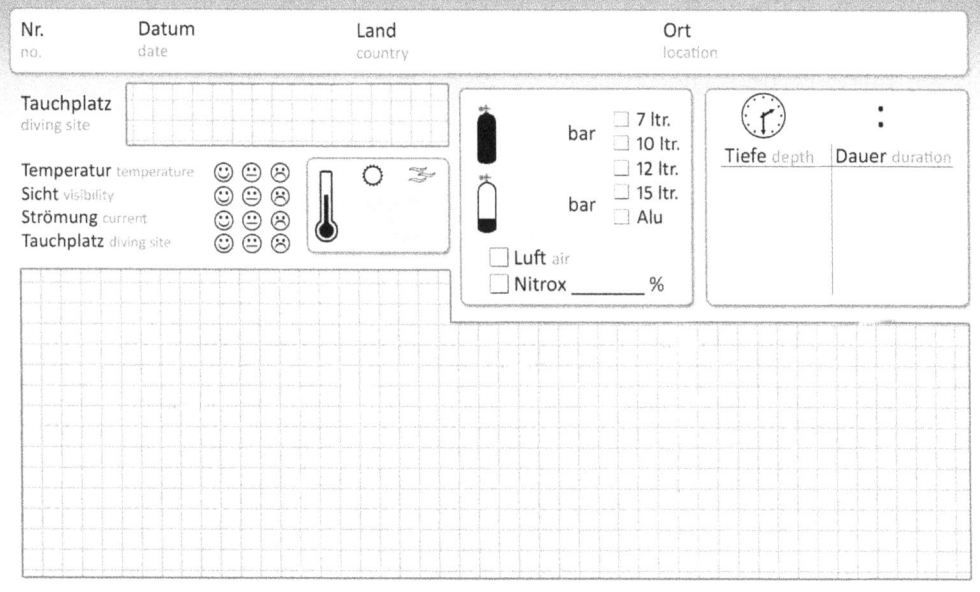

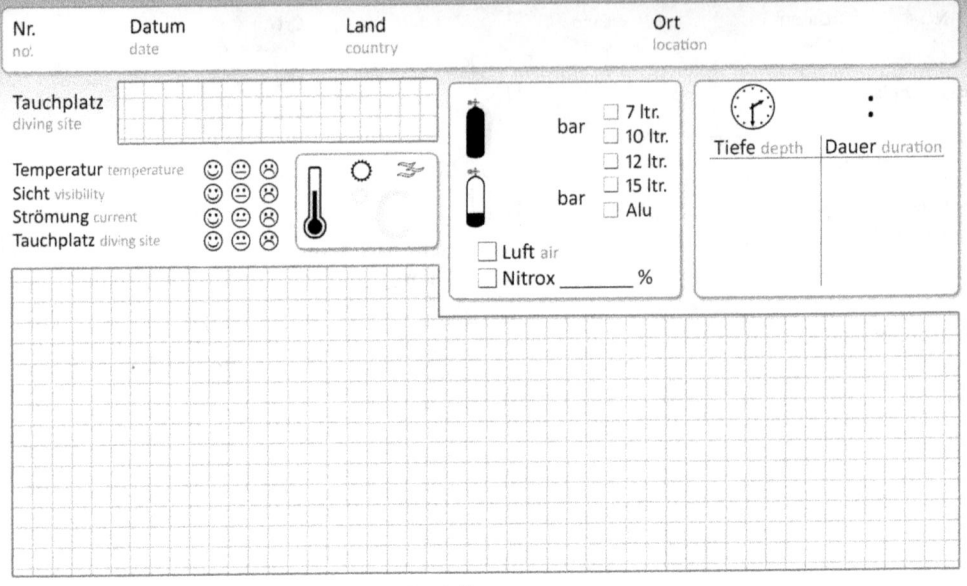
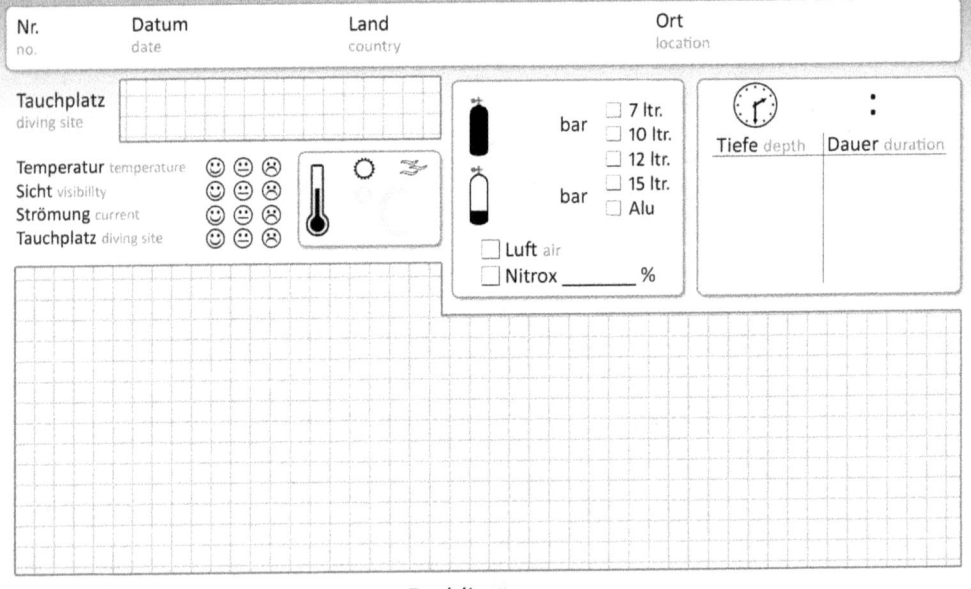

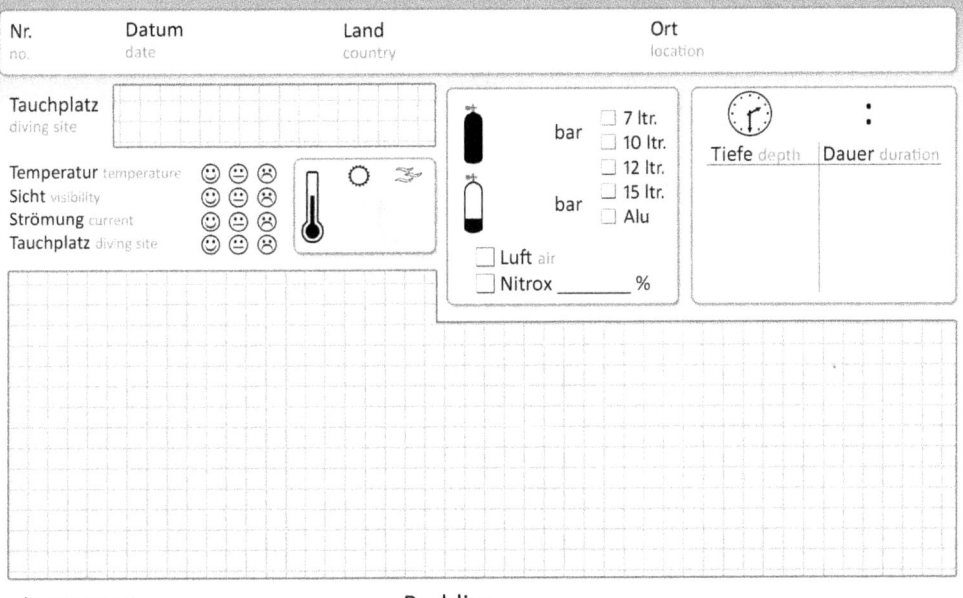

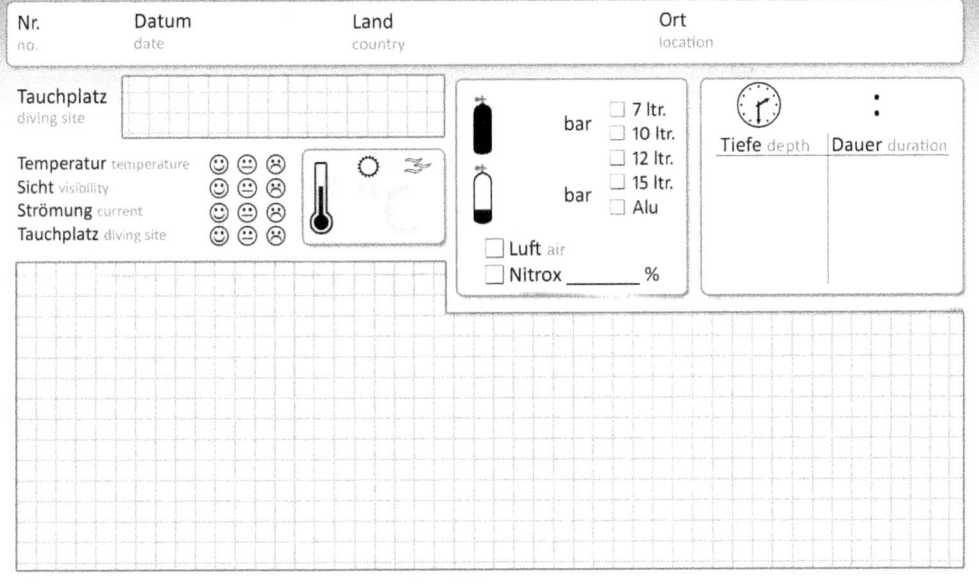

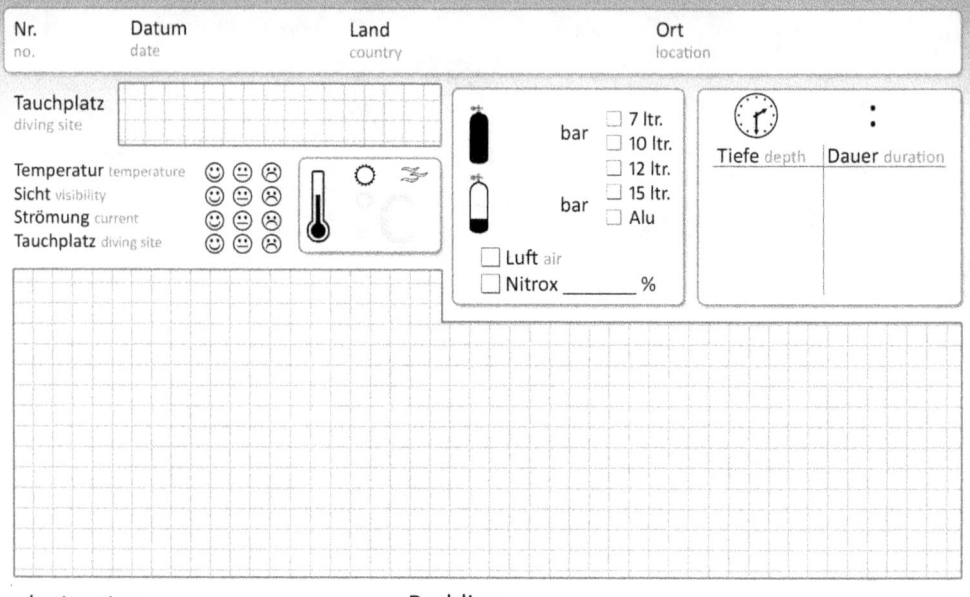

Instructor Buddies
Signature:

No.:

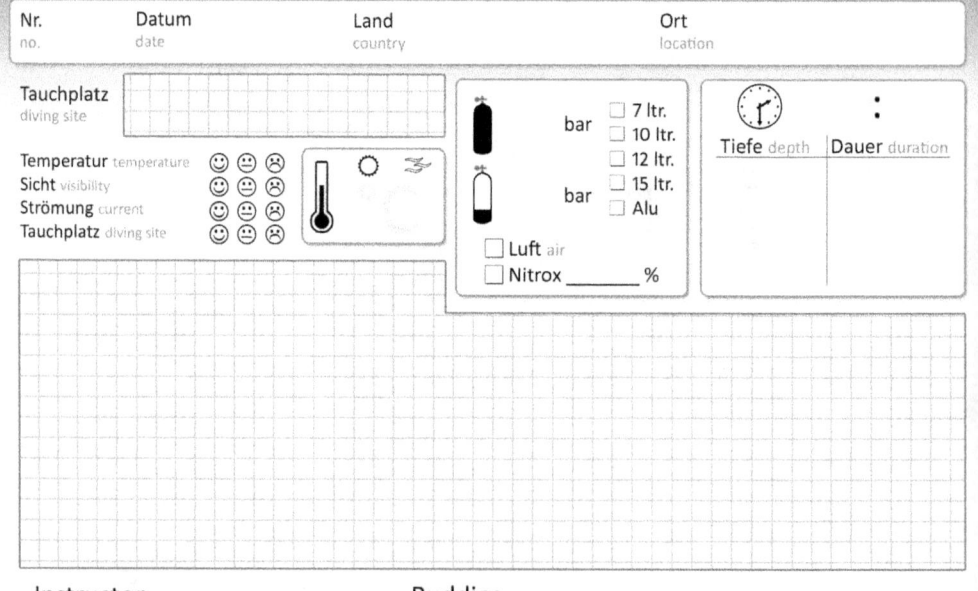

Instructor Buddies
Signature:

No.:

Nr. no.	Datum date	Land country	Ort location

Tauchplatz diving site

Temperatur temperature ☺ 😐 ☹
Sicht visibility ☺ 😐 ☹
Strömung current ☺ 😐 ☹
Tauchplatz diving site ☺ 😐 ☹

bar
☐ 7 ltr.
☐ 10 ltr.
☐ 12 ltr.
bar ☐ 15 ltr.
☐ Alu

☐ Luft air
☐ Nitrox _____ %

Tiefe depth	Dauer duration

Instructor   Buddies
Signature:

No.:

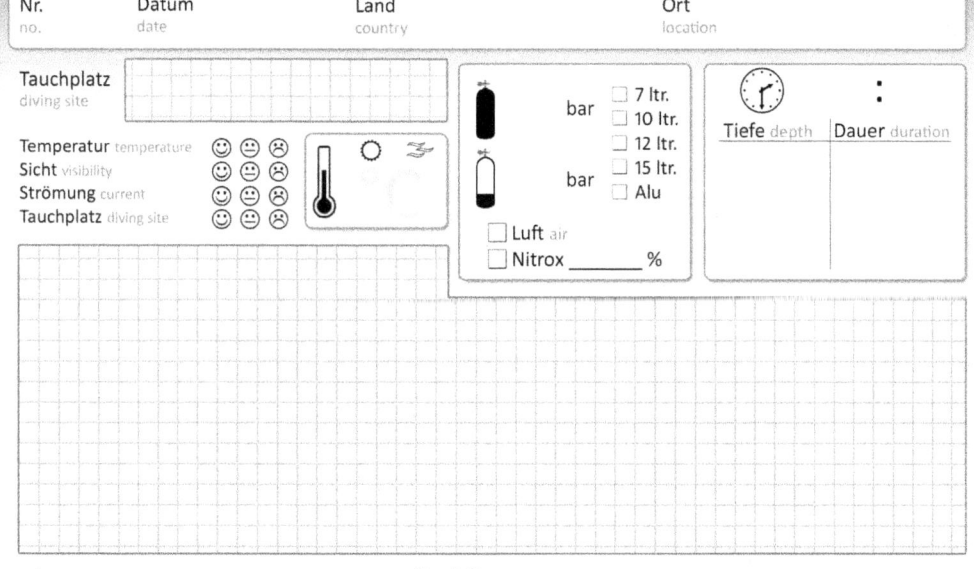

Nr. no.	Datum date	Land country	Ort location

Tauchplatz diving site

Temperatur temperature ☺ 😐 ☹
Sicht visibility ☺ 😐 ☹
Strömung current ☺ 😐 ☹
Tauchplatz diving site ☺ 😐 ☹

bar
☐ 7 ltr.
☐ 10 ltr.
☐ 12 ltr.
bar ☐ 15 ltr.
☐ Alu

☐ Luft air
☐ Nitrox _____ %

Tiefe depth	Dauer duration

Instructor   Buddies
Signature:

No.:

Buddy-Liste buddy-list

Name / name	Notizen / notes	Stempel / stamp
Kontakt / contact information		

Name / name	Notizen / notes	Stempel / stamp
Kontakt / contact information		

Name / name	Notizen / notes	Stempel / stamp
Kontakt / contact information		

Name / name	Notizen / notes	Stempel / stamp
Kontakt / contact information		

Name / name	Notizen / notes	Stempel / stamp
Kontakt / contact information		

Name / name	Notizen / notes	Stempel / stamp
Kontakt / contact information		

Buddy-Liste buddy-list

Name
name
Kontakt
contact
information

Notizen
notes

Stempel
stamp

Name
name
Kontakt
contact
information

Notizen
notes

Stempel
stamp

Name
name
Kontakt
contact
information

Notizen
notes

Stempel
stamp

Name
name
Kontakt
contact
information

Notizen
notes

Stempel
stamp

Name
name
Kontakt
contact
information

Notizen
notes

Stempel
stamp

Name
name
Kontakt
contact
information

Notizen
notes

Stempel
stamp

Buddy-Liste buddy-list

Name / name
Kontakt / contact information

Notizen / notes

Stempel / stamp

Name / name
Kontakt / contact information

Notizen / notes

Stempel / stamp

Name / name
Kontakt / contact information

Notizen / notes

Stempel / stamp

Name / name
Kontakt / contact information

Notizen / notes

Stempel / stamp

Name / name
Kontakt / contact information

Notizen / notes

Stempel / stamp

Name / name
Kontakt / contact information

Notizen / notes

Stempel / stamp

Buddy-Liste buddy-list

Name / name
Kontakt / contact information

Notizen / notes

Stempel / stamp

Name / name
Kontakt / contact information

Notizen / notes

Stempel / stamp

Name / name
Kontakt / contact information

Notizen / notes

Stempel / stamp

Name / name
Kontakt / contact information

Notizen / notes

Stempel / stamp

Name / name
Kontakt / contact information

Notizen / notes

Stempel / stamp

Name / name
Kontakt / contact information

Notizen / notes

Stempel / stamp

Buddy-Liste buddy-list

Name
name
Kontakt
contact
information

Notizen
notes

Stempel
stamp

Name
name
Kontakt
contact
information

Notizen
notes

Stempel
stamp

Name
name
Kontakt
contact
information

Notizen
notes

Stempel
stamp

Name
name
Kontakt
contact
information

Notizen
notes

Stempel
stamp

Name
name
Kontakt
contact
information

Notizen
notes

Stempel
stamp

Name
name
Kontakt
contact
information

Notizen
notes

Stempel
stamp

Notizen notes

Notizen notes

www.ingramcontent.com/pod-product-compliance
Lightning Source LLC
Chambersburg PA
CBHW061449040426
42450CB00007B/1281